THE
LION
OF JUDAH

THE LION OF JUDAH

*He will not come as a lamb
but a judge of the earth*

Philip Odei Tettey

The lion of judah

Copyright © 2020 by Philip Odei Tettey. All rights reserved.

No part of this publication may be reproduced, stored in a retrieval system or transmitted in any way by any means, electronic, mechanical, photocopy, recording or otherwise without the prior permission of the author except as provided by USA copyright law.

The opinions expressed by the author are not necessarily those of URLink Print and Media.

1603 Capitol Ave., Suite 310 Cheyenne, Wyoming USA 82001
1-888-980-6523 | admin@urlinkpublishing.com

URLink Print and Media is committed to excellence in the publishing industry.

Book design copyright © 2020 by URLink Print and Media. All rights reserved.

Published in the United States of America

ISBN 978-1-64753-379-3 (Paperback)
ISBN 978-1-64753-380-9 (Digital)

28.05.20

My name is Philip Odei Tettey, am very happy to dedicate this book to my loving wife Cristina Tettey.

Achievements

B.Sc. In Mechanical Engineering, Diploma in Refrigeration & Air-Conditioning, Accra, Ghana.

Associate in Business Program i Information Technology at American Inter- Continental University, Illinois, USA.

Masters in International Business Administration, University of Liverpool, UK.

Diploma in Accounting & Finance at Dublin Business, Rep. of Ireland.

An Elder of the Church of Pentecost, Rep. of Ireland.

He will not come as a lamb again but as the lion of Judah and judge of all mankind on earth.

The history of the tribe of Judah, which eventually became a nation, begins in the book of Genesis. Judah was the fourth son of the patriarch Jacob by his first wife, Leah Genesis 29:35. He grew up with his brothers, working in the family business tending cattle and sheep.

In time Judah and his brothers developed hatred from jealousy and envy of their younger brother Joseph. Joseph was favoured by his father, who gave him a special coat Genesis 37:3. But it was when Joseph told his brothers about his dreams, which indicated he would be greater than them, that their hatred of him intensified verses 5-11.

The hatred grew to the point that the brothers wanted to actually kill Joseph; but Reuben, the firstborn, stepped in to stop them. Joseph was placed in a pit; and while Reuben was absent, Judah came up with the idea of selling Joseph to Midianite traders for 20 shekels of silver verses 18-22, 26-29. The brothers killed a goat and covered Joseph's coat with blood to deceive their father into believing a wild animal had killed him. Jacob could never get over his grief for the loss of his son Genesis 37:35.

Judah suffers with family problems

Judah and his brothers thought they had taken care of the problem of their younger brother, but God did not let that be the end of the story. Judah's family would suffer many trials over the next 20 years or more. Judah married a Canaanite woman named Shua. They had three sons, Er, Onan and Shelah.

Judah took a wife, Tamar, for his firstborn son, Er, but he was so evil that God took his life Genesis 38:6-7. Judah commanded his second-born son, Onan, to marry Tamar and produce an heir for his deceased brother as God's laws commanded in such circumstances. Onan would not carry through with this act because it would not be his heir. God then took Onan's life for his refusal to give his brother an heir Genesis 38:8-10.

A strange event in Judah's life

Following Onan's death, Judah asked Tamar to not remarry, but to wait in her father's house until Judah's youngest son, Shelah, was old enough to marry. Tamar complied with Judah's wishes. But quite a number of years went by, and Judah's wife, Shua, died. Tamar realized that she was not going to be given in marriage to Shelah, who was now grown Genesis 38:11-14.

One day Tamar heard that her father-in-law was heading out to shear his sheep. She removed her widow's garments and dressed to appear as a harlot as she sat along the road where Judah would pass by. Judah did not recognize her and propositioned her; and she demanded his signet, cord and staff for collateral. When it was later discovered that she was pregnant, Judah threatened her with death for harlotry. To save her life, she presented the items belonging to Judah and said, "By the man to whom these belong, I am with child Genesis 38:18, 24-26.

Tamar had twins. At delivery, one twin put out his hand first and the midwife tied a scarlet thread on it and said, "This one came out first." But the other twin, Perez, came out unexpectedly followed by Zerah with the scarlet thread tied on his hand Genesis 38:27-30. God would use the unusual birth of these twins to establish two lines of genealogy in the tribe of Judah.

The second great promise God gave to Abraham stated, "And in you all the families of the earth shall be blessed Genesis 12:3. This promise would come through the line of Perez. King David and the kings of Judah would descend through the line of Perez. But most importantly, Jesus Christ would come through this line so "all the families of the earth shall be blessed Matthew 1:3, 16.

Why the tribe of Judah?

In looking at the life of Judah and his character, it is hard to see why the tribe of Judah should become so prominent among the tribes of Israel. On the one hand, Joseph lived a righteous life and was blessed with the birth right in place of Reuben, the firstborn. The name of Israel was passed on to his two sons, Ephraim and Manasseh. Yet God also chose Judah and his descendants for a special place in His plan through the ages. The prophecy God gave to Jacob at the end of his life concerning his sons' descendants in the latter days reveals a special blessing for the tribe of Judah Genesis 49:1, 8-10.

In speaking of the tribe of Judah, Jacob said, "Judah, you are he whom your brothers shall praise; your hand shall be on the neck of your enemies; your father's children shall bow down before you. Judah is a lion's whelp; from the prey, my son, you have gone up. He bows down; he lies down as a lion; and as a lion, which shall rouse him? The scepter shall not depart from Judah, nor a lawgiver from between his feet, until Shiloh comes; and to Him shall be the obedience of the people" Genesis 49:8-10.

In this passage God looked at Judah as a strong warrior and likened him to a young lion sleeping in its den after devouring its prey. Perhaps it was this strength of character and determination that God foresaw in this tribe that influenced Him to choose Judah to be His lawgiver and the tribe from which His Son would later be born Hebrews 7:14.

Regarding Genesis 49:10, Expositor's Bible Commentary says, "The word 'Shiloh,' found in some English versions, is simply a translated form of the Hebrew expression meaning 'one to whom it belongs. Jesus Christ is the one to whom it belongs.

David was apparently inspired by this passage in Genesis 49 to twice say in the Psalms that Judah is my lawgiver Psalms 60:7; 108:8.

The tribe of Judah has not only been a lawgiver, but a preserver of God's written laws. The apostle Paul said what advantage then has the Jew? Much in every way! Chiefly because to them were committed the oracles that which was spoken or commanded of God Romans 3:1-2. Through the centuries, the Jews have faithfully preserved the books of the Old Testament and the Hebrew calendar.

Judah prevails over his brothers

The postexilic writer of 1 Chronicles, probably Ezra, wrote, Yet Judah prevailed over his brothers, and from him came a ruler, although the birth right was Joseph's 1 Chronicles 5:2.

How did Judah prevail?

During the time of Moses, the tribe of Judah became the stronger tribe and prevailed over his brothers. The census in Numbers 1 shows that Judah was the leading tribe in population and in men who could go to war Numbers 1:2-3, 27.

After the death of Joshua, God chose the tribe of Judah to take the lead in conquering the nations who were living in the land promised to the 12 tribes Judges 1:2. The first chapter of Judges shows that the tribe of Judah was aggressive and strong in driving out the Canaanites in the southern half of the land of Canaan.

The good news for the tribe of Judah and this world is that the Lion of the tribe of Judah, Jesus Christ, will return to establish the Kingdom of God, and the tribe of Judah will finally accept its Redeemer. An even more important way that Judah prevailed over his brothers took place during the time of King David. The tabernacle of God had long been in Shiloh in the territory of Joseph. But David set the stage for the temple to be built on Mount Zion, which He God loved, in the tribe of Judah Psalm 78:67-70. God chose David to be His shepherd and Jerusalem Mount Zion for His place to dwell. God also chose David to hold the "sceptre," a symbol of kingship that would always remain in the tribe of Judah Genesis 49:10; Psalm 89:34-37.

National captivity

After the death of Solomon, the nation of Israel became divided. Solomon's son Rehoboam refused to lighten the burden of taxes that had been imposed by his father. In fact, Rehoboam threatened to make life far worse for the people than what his father had done. This resulted in 10 tribes separating and becoming the northern kingdom of Israel with its capital city in Samaria 1 Kings 12:12-14. The tribes of Judah, Benjamin and a part of Levi stayed with Rehoboam and became the southern kingdom of Judah, with Jerusalem as its capital.

The northern kingdom of Israel immediately went into idolatry and turned away from worshipping God. After 200 years, they went into national captivity at the hands of the Assyrian Empire.

The southern kingdom of Judah lasted more than a hundred years after the fall of the northern kingdom of Israel. Judah also turned away from the God of their fathers and went after idols several times, and several times righteous kings instituted reforms. God sent prophets to warn them of their slide into idolatry, but eventually they would no longer listen. The Jewish nation was taken into national captivity by the Babylonians in several waves of deportations culminating in 586 B.C.

End-time nationhood

After 70 years of captivity in Babylon, some of the Jews returned to Jerusalem to rebuild the temple, but they didn't fully return to the status of a sovereign nation until the 20th century. Jesus the Messiah, the Saviour of mankind would come through the tribe of Judah, but He would be rejected by His own people. The Church Jesus established initially sprang out of the tribe of Judah. But since the middle of the first century, the Church of God has become largely non-Jewish in membership.

Approaching the 20th century, many Jewish groups and Christian churches were advocating a homeland in Palestine for the tribe of Judah. Jewish groups wanted to return to Judea because it was their ancient homeland. Christian groups saw the establishment of a Jewish state as a sign of end-time prophecy being fulfilled that would lead to the imminent return of Jesus Christ. One such prophecy can be found in Daniel 12:11, which indicates that the Jews will resume animal sacrifices before the return of Christ. Presumably, they would need their own homeland to do this.

In 1917 the Balfour Declaration made public Great Britain's support of a Jewish homeland in Palestine. But it would not become a reality until May 14, 1948. Today, the nation called Israel is a major power in the Middle East, but will it remain such a power until the second coming of Jesus Christ?

Tribulation and restoration

Jesus in His Olivet Prophecy said, For then there will be great tribulation, such as has not been since the beginning of the world until this time, no, nor ever shall be Matthew 24:21. The tribe of Judah and the State of Israel will not be spared from this traumatic time. In Luke's account of the same prophecy, Jesus said, but when you see Jerusalem surrounded by armies, and then know that its desolation is near Luke 21:20.

The prophet Zechariah also spoke of this same time, "For I will gather all the nations to battle against Jerusalem; the city shall be taken, the houses rifled, and the women ravished. Half of the city shall go into captivity, but the remnant of the people shall not be cut off from the city Zechariah 14:2. Invasion and war will come to Jerusalem and to the tribe of Judah.

Following the prophecy of the invasion of Israel and Jerusalem, Zechariah announced the good news of the coming of Christ: And in that day His feet will stand on the Mount of Olives. And the LORD shall be King over all the earth" Zechariah 14:4, 9.

Jeremiah spoke of this same time when he said, In His days Judah will be saved, and Israel will dwell safely; now this is His name by which He will be called: **THE LORD OUR RIGHTEOUSNESS** Jeremiah 23:6.

The good news for the tribe of Judah and this world is that the "Lion of the tribe of Judah, Jesus Christ Revelation 5:5, will return to establish the Kingdom of God, and the tribe of Judah will finally accept its Redeemer Romans 11:26.

Read more about this wonderful promised future in the section on the "Kingdom of God." You can also find related articles in this section about the "12 Tribes of Israel" and the section about the "Middle East in Bible Prophecy."

The Twelve Tribes of Israel

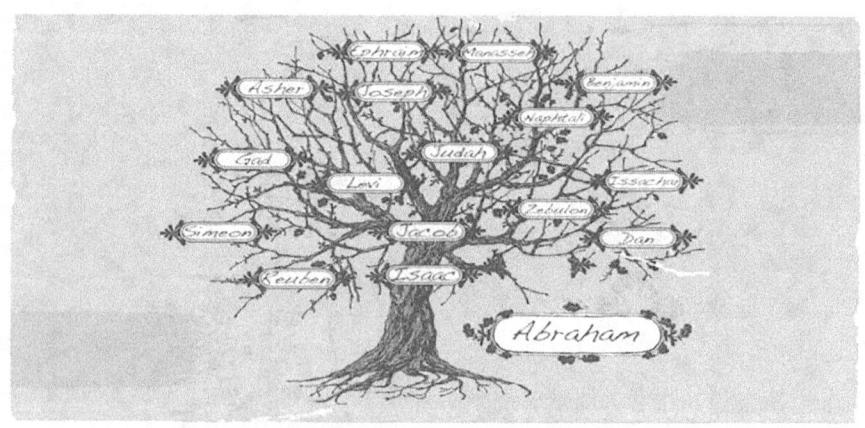

The Scriptures are quite clear that among all the nations in the world, God chose Israel as the one He would work with. This was the nation that God delivered out of slavery in Egypt, the nation to whom God gave the land of Canaan, and the nation through whom would come Jesus, the Messiah. Was there something special about these people unlike others?

God Himself answered this very question. In addressing the ancient Israelites, He told them: "For you are a holy people to the LORD your God; the LORD your God has chosen you to be a people for Him, a special treasure above all the peoples on the face of the earth. The LORD did not set His love on you nor choose you because you were more in number than any other people, for you were the least of all peoples; but because the LORD loves you, and because He would keep the oath which He swore to your fathers, the LORD has brought you out with a mighty hand, and redeemed you from the house of bondage, from the hand of Pharaoh king of Egypt Deuteronomy 7:6-8, emphasis added.

So why did God choose Israel? God chose the ancient Israelites because He had promised Abraham that his descendants would become a great nation and occupy the land of Canaan (Genesis 12:3, 7; 17:4, 7-8; 22:17). God blessed Abraham and his descendants because of Abraham's faith, a living faith that resulted in diligent obedience to God's instructions and law (Genesis 26:3-5). This promise was repeated to Abraham's son, Isaac, and to Abraham's grandson, Jacob (Genesis 17:21; 26:24; 28:1-4, 13).

God's purpose in choosing Israel was for them to be a model nation to other nations and that through them "all the families of the earth" would be blessed (Genesis 12:3). He wanted Israel to be "a kingdom of priests and a holy nation" (Exodus 19:6). Other nations would see that when the Israelites obeyed God, they were blessed (verse 5), and when they disobeyed God, they would be punished in Deuteronomy

The Bible lists 12 sons of the patriarch Israel who each became the father of a tribe of the ancient nation of Israel. Here is a list of the 12 tribes of Israel from Genesis 49:

Reuben & Simeon.

Levi (this priestly tribe did not receive a territory, and sometimes is not listed when the tribe of Joseph is listed as two separate tribes).

Judah, Zebulun, Issachar, Dan. Gad. Asher. Naphtali.

Joseph often listed as two tribes named for his sons, Ephraim and Manasseh.

Benjamin.

Let's look at what the Bible tells us about the history and the future of the 12 tribes of Israel.

Promises made to Abraham, Isaac and Jacob God promised Abraham that his descendants would be numerous (Genesis 13:16; 17:2; 22:17) and that his descendants would eventually constitute "many nations" (Genesis 17:4-5). He also promised Abraham that his descendants would "possess the gate of their enemies" (Genesis 22:17) and be "blessed" mightily by God (verses 16-18).

God also said that his descendants would be identified throughout history by the name of Abraham's son, "Isaac" (Genesis 21:12). The blessings given to Abraham and Isaac were called the "birth right" blessings because they were passed on to successive generations as a right of their birth.

The "birth right" blessings given to Abraham were passed on to Isaac, who married Rebekah. Millions of people would descend from Isaac and Rebekah over time. In fact, they would number in the billions throughout the generations of humanity on the earth.

The blessing of numerous descendants who would possess the gates of their enemies was a continuation of the blessing God had promised Abraham that He would fulfil in Isaac (Genesis 17:17-19, 21). However, Abraham had a previous son, Ishmael, by Hagar, and Ishmael's descendants were also prophesied to become numerous and constitute a "great nation" that would feature "twelve princes" (verse 20).

The "great nation" of Ishmael's descendants today is the Arab world. The Arabs know that they are descended from Ishmael, the son of Abraham and Hagar.

If the descendants of Ishmael constitute the Arabs, the peoples who make up most of the nations in the modern Middle East, then which nations descended from Isaac? If the Bible is true, Isaac's descendants should constitute nations more numerous, prosperous and powerful than the Arabs. The Bible is God's truth (John 17:17)! Obviously, Isaac's descendants in the modern world must consist of far more than just the Jews. Genesis 24:60 prophesied that Isaac's descendants would number in the multiple millions over time.

Isaac passed his "birth right" blessings on to his son, Jacob, even though the oldest son, Esau, would normally have received them. Genesis 25:30-34 informs us that Esau "sold" his birth right to Jacob for some red stew. Then when their father, Isaac, officially passed on the birth right, Jacob deceived his father into believing he was his brother. In essence, Jacob "stole" the birth right through deception (Genesis 27).

One of the blessings Jacob received from Isaac was that other nations would bow down to the nations that would descend from Jacob (Genesis 27:29). Clearly, for this prophecy to be fulfilled, Jacob's descendants would have to become great nations and empires. This same blessing also promised that God would bless the nations that blessed Jacob's descendants and would curse the nations that cursed Jacob's descendants.

God reiterated Abraham's blessings to Jacob in Genesis 28:10-15 by saying Jacob's descendants would be as numerous as "the dust of the earth" and they would eventually spread to all four corners of the earth from the region of the Promised Land. Jacob's name was later changed to "Israel" (Genesis 32:28), and he had 12 sons who became the "12 tribes of Israel."

The 12 tribes of Israel established

Before Jacob Israel died, he passed on the "birth right blessings" to his grandsons, who were named Ephraim and Manasseh. Israel gave prophetic blessings that were to be fulfilled in a time called "the last days" to all 12 of his sons (Genesis 49:1).

In Genesis 48:16, Israel blessed both Ephraim and Manasseh simultaneously with the words "let my name be named on them, and the name of my father's Abraham and Isaac; and let them grow into a multitude in the midst of the earth." Israel decreed that his own name, "Israel," and the name of his own father, "Isaac," would be placed upon the descendants of Ephraim and Manasseh, the two sons of Joseph, who were to each become a distinct tribe among Israel's sons (Genesis 48:5). In doing this, Israel was giving Joseph a "double portion" among the 12 tribes of Israel.

Israel foretold in Genesis 48:19 that while the descendants of Manasseh would become a "great" people or nation, the descendants of Ephraim would become a "multitude of nations." Since Joseph was expanded into two tribes, this meant that there would now be 13 tribes of Israel, although they were often still known as "the 12 tribes of Israel" because the priestly tribe, the Levites, did not receive a territorial inheritance in the Promised Land.

In the blessings recorded in Genesis 49, Israel gave prophecies for each of the tribes named after his 12 sons. The 12 sons of Israel are Reuben, Simeon, Levi, Judah, Zebulun, Issachar, Dan, Gad, Asher, Naphtali, Joseph and Benjamin. The tribe most recognized by modern readers is Judah. Judah's descendants have long been called "Jews." However, Judah is just one of the sons of Israel. The vast majority of Israel's descendants came from the other sons who were not called Jews.

The rise and fall of the 12 tribes of Israel

When the 12 tribes of Israel entered the Promised Land, they eventually formed the nation of Israel under David and Solomon. Soon after Solomon's death, this empire was torn apart by a great civil war. The northern 10 tribes formed the kingdom of Israel, while the southern two tribes, Judah and Benjamin joined by the priestly tribe of Levi, formed the southern kingdom of Judah. The northern kingdom of Israel was called "Israel" because it was led by the tribes of Ephraim and Manasseh who bore the name of "Israel" (Genesis 48:16). The southern kingdom was led by the tribe of Judah.

The kingdoms of Israel and Judah became enemies and often fought bloody wars. Though they have not reunited, they are prophesied to do so in the future. See "Israel and Judah: When Will They Be Reunited?"

The northern kingdom of Israel went into captivity in 722 B.C. because of sin and rebellion toward God. Judah was taken into captivity by the Babylonians between 604 and 586 B.C.

Just before the fall of Israel, the prophet Amos noted that the northern 10 tribes were known by the name "house of Isaac" (Amos 7:16) just as the prophecies of Genesis 21:12 and 48:16 had predicted. The name of "Isaac" followed the 10 tribes wherever they went in their exile and later migrations.

In Jeremiah 51:5, we find a prophecy, given over a century after the 10 tribes went into captivity, that they would not be forsaken by God. Though sometimes called the "10 Lost Tribes of Israel," these peoples are not lost to God or to students of the Bible who understand how to trace their history. To understand who some of these peoples are today, see "12 Tribes of Israel Today: Who Are They?" and "Who Are the United States and Britain in Prophecy?"

Modern significance of the 12 tribes of Israel

The 12 tribes of Israel eventually grew into great nations and empires just as God had predicted. Identifying these nations today helps us understand what will occur before Christ's return.

Some people mistakenly think that, since the establishment of the New Testament Church, the identities of these people no longer serve any purpose. The truth is that God has many more plans for the peoples who have descended from the 12 tribes of Israel after Christ returns. For additional information, be sure to read the related articles on this site.

Promises made to Abraham, Isaac and Jacob

God promised Abraham that his descendants would be numerous (Genesis 13:16; 17:2; 22:17) and that his descendants would eventually constitute "many nations" (Genesis 17:4-5). He also promised Abraham that his descendants would "possess the gate of their enemies" (Genesis 22:17) and be "blessed" mightily by God (verses 16-18).

God also said that his descendants would be identified throughout history by the name of Abraham's son, "Isaac" (Genesis 21:12). The blessings given to Abraham and Isaac were called the "birth right" blessings because they were passed on to successive generations as a right of their birth.

The "birthright" blessings given to Abraham were passed on to Isaac, who married Rebekah. Millions of people would descend from Isaac and Rebekah over time. In fact, they would number in the billions throughout the generations of humanity on the earth.

The blessing of numerous descendants who would possess the gates of their enemies was a continuation of the blessing God had promised Abraham that He would fulfil in Isaac (Genesis 17:17-19, 21). However, Abraham had a previous son, Ishmael, by Hagar, and

Ishmael's descendants were also prophesied to become numerous and constitute a "great nation" that would feature "twelve princes verse 20.

The "great nation of Ishmael's descendants today is the Arab world. The Arabs know that they are descended from Ishmael, the son of Abraham and Hagar.

If the descendants of Ishmael constitute the Arabs, the peoples who make up most of the nations in the modern Middle East, then which nations descended from Isaac? If the Bible is true, Isaac's descendants should constitute nations more numerous, prosperous and powerful than the Arabs. The Bible is God's truth (John 17:17)! Obviously, Isaac's descendants in the modern world must consist of far more than just the Jews. Genesis 24:60 prophesied that Isaac's descendants would number in the multiple millions over time.

Isaac passed his "birth right" blessings on to his son, Jacob, even though the oldest son, Esau, would normally have received them. Genesis 25:30-34.

One of the blessings Jacob received from Isaac was that other nations would bow down to the nations that would descend from Jacob (Genesis 27:29). Clearly, for this prophecy to be fulfilled, Jacob's descendants would have to become great nations and empires. This same blessing also promised that God would bless the nations that blessed Jacob's descendants and would curse the nations that cursed Jacob's descendants.

God reiterated Abraham's blessings to Jacob in Genesis 28:10-15 by saying Jacob's descendants would be as numerous as "the dust of the earth" and they would eventually spread to all four corners of the earth from the region of the Promised Land. Jacob's name was later changed to "Israel" (Genesis 32:28), and he had 12 sons who became the "12 tribes of Israel."

Israel foretold in Genesis 48:19 that while the descendants of Manasseh would become a "great" people (or nation), the descendants of Ephraim would become a "multitude of nations." Since Joseph was expanded into two tribes, this meant that there would now be 13 tribes of Israel, although they were often still known as "the 12 tribes of Israel" because the priestly tribe, the Levites, did not receive a territorial inheritance in the Promised Land.

The kingdoms of Israel and Judah became enemies and often fought bloody wars. Though they have not reunited, they are prophesied to do so in the future. See "Israel and Judah: When Will They Be Reunited?"

Modern significance of the 12 tribes of Israel

The 12 tribes of Israel eventually grew into great nations and empires just as God had predicted. Identifying these nations today helps us understand what will occur before Christ's return. Some people mistakenly think that, since the establishment of the New Testament Church, the identities of these people no longer serve any purpose. The truth is that God has many more plans for the peoples who have descended from the 12 tribes of Israel after Christ returns. For additional information, be sure to read the related articles on this site.

Parallel Verses

New International Version Then one of the elders said to me, "Do not weep! See, the Lion of the tribe of Judah, the Root of David, has triumphed. He is able to open the scroll and its seven seals."

New Living Translation

But one of the twenty-four elders said to me, "Stop weeping! Look, the Lion of the tribe of Judah, the heir to David's throne, has won the victory. He is worthy to open the scroll and its seven seals. "English Standard Version And one of the elders said to me, "Weep no more; behold, the Lion of the tribe of Judah, the Root of David, has conquered, so that he can open the scroll and its seven seals. Then one of the elders said to me, do not weep! Behold, the Lion of the tribe of Judah, the root of David, has triumphed to open the scroll and its seven seals. "And one of the elders says to me, do not weep. Behold, the Lion of the tribe of Judah, the root of David, has overcome to open the scroll and its seven seals."

New American Standard Bible and one of the elders said to me, "Stop weeping; behold, the Lion that is from the tribe of Judah, the Root of David, has overcome so as to open the book and its seven seals."

King James Bible And one of the elders said unto me, weep not: behold, the Lion of the tribe of Judah, the Root of David, hath prevailed to open the book, and to lose the seven seals thereof.

Then one of the elders said to me, Stop crying. Look! The Lion from the tribe of Judah, the Root of David, has been victorious so that He may open the scroll and its seven seals."

International Standard Version "Stop crying," one of the elders told me. "Look! The Lion from the tribe of Judah, the Root of David, has conquered. He can open the scroll and its seven seals."

American King James Version

And one of the elders said to me, Weep not: behold, the Lion of the tribe of Judah, the Root of David, has prevailed to open the book, and to lose the seven seals thereof.

And one of the elders says to me, do not weep. Behold, the lion which [is] of the tribe of Judah, the root of David, has overcome [so as] to open the book, and its seven seals.

THE LION OF JUDAH

Webster's Bible Translation

And one of the elders said to me, Weep not: behold, the Lion of the tribe of Judah, the Root of David, hath prevailed to open the book, and to lose its seven seals. Matthew Henry Commentary 5:1-7 the apostle saw in the hand of Him that sat upon the throne, a roll of parchments in the form usual in those times, and sealed with seven seals. This represented the secret purposes of God about to be revealed. The designs and methods of Divine Providence, toward the church and the world, are stated, fixed, and made a matter of record. The counsels of God are altogether hidden from the eye and understanding of the creature. The several parts are not unsealed and opened at once, but after each other, till the whole mystery of God's counsel and conduct is finished in the world. The creatures cannot open it, nor read it; the Lord only can do so. Those who see most of God, are most desirous to see more; and those who have seen his glory, desire to know his will. But even good men may be too eager and hasty to look into the mysteries of the Divine conduct. Such desires, if not soon answered, turn to grief and sorrow. If John wept much because he could not look into the book of God's decrees, what reason have many to shed floods of tears for their ignorance of the gospel of Christ! Of that on which everlasting salvation depends! We need not weep that we cannot foresee future events respecting ourselves in this world; the eager expectation of future prospects, or the foresight of future calamities, would alike unfit us for present duties and conflicts, or render our prosperous days distressing. Yet we may desire to learn, from the promises and prophecies of Scripture, what will be the final event to believers and to the church; and the Incarnate Son has prevailed, that we should learn all that we need to know. Christ stands as Mediator between God and both ministers and people. He is called a Lion, but he appears as a Lamb slain. He appears with the marks of his sufferings, to show that he pleads for us in heaven, in virtue of his satisfaction. He appears as a Lamb, having seven horns and seven eyes; perfect power to execute all the will of God, and perfect wisdom to understand it, and to do it in the most effectual manner. The Father put the book of his eternal counsels into the hand of Christ, and Christ readily and gladly took it into his hand; for he delights to make known the will of his Father; and the Holy Spirit is given by him to reveal the truth and will of God

Study Bible

The Lamb is Worthy

4And I began to weep bitterly, because no one was found worthy to open the scroll or look inside it. 5Then one of the elders said to me, "Do not weep! Behold, the Lion of the tribe of Judah, the root of David, has triumphed to open the scroll and its seven seals." 6Then I saw a Lamb who appeared to have been slain, standing in the centre of the throne, encircled by the four living creatures and the elders. The lamb had seven horns and seven eyes, which represent the sevenfold Spirit of God sent out into all the earth

Cross References

Genesis 49:9

"Judah is a lion's whelp; from the prey, my son, you have gone up. He couches, he lies down as a lion, And as a lion, who dares rouse him up?

Isaiah 11:1 Then a shoot will spring from the stem of Jesse, and a branch from his roots will bear fruit.

Isaiah 11:10 Then in that day the nations will resort to the root of Jesse, Who will stand as a signal for the peoples; and His resting place will be glorious.

Daniel 7:16 "I approached one of those who were standing by and began asking him the exact meaning of all this. So he told me and made known to me the interpretation of these things:

Romans 15:12 And once more, Isaiah says: "The root of Jesse will appear, One who will arise to rule over the Gentiles; in Him the Gentiles will put their hope."

Hebrews 7:14 for it is clear that our Lord descended from Judah, a tribe as to which Moses said nothing about priests.

Revelation 3:21 To the one who is victorious, I will grant the right to sit with Me on My throne, just as I overcame and sat down with My Father on His throne.

Revelation 5:4 And I began to weep bitterly, because no one was found worthy to open the scroll or look inside it.

Revelation 22:16 "I, Jesus, have sent my angel to give you this testimony for the churches. I am the Root and the Offspring of David, the bright Morning Star."

Treasury of Scripture and one of the elders said to me, Weep not: behold, the Lion of the tribe of Judah, the Root of David, has prevailed to open the book, and to lose the seven seals thereof.

Revelation 4:4, 10 and round about the throne were four and twenty seats: and on the …

Revelation 7:13 and one of the elders answered, saying to me, what are these which …

Jeremiah 31:16 thus said the LORD; Refrain your voice from weeping, and your eyes …

Luke 7:13 and when the Lord saw her, he had compassion on her, and said to her, Weep not.

Luke 8:52 and all wept, and bewailed her: but he said, Weep not; she is not …

JESUS CHRIST is our Savior and Redeemer and the Only Begotten Son of God the Father, When we submit to Jesus Christ's transformative influence, we become humble and teachable, and we recognize the divine Light of Christ inside each of us.

The world knows that 2,000 years ago a man named Jesus came from the town of Nazareth in what is now called Israel. He traveled about the region and gained a large followers. After a few years, the religious leaders in Jerusalem falsely accused him of crimes and handed him over to the Roman authorities. They executed him by nailing him to a cross. A short time later, his followers preached in the name of Jesus Christ, whom they said rose from the dead. More and more followers were added to this movement which has become the Christian church of today.

These are the facts upon which even the greatest skeptic will agree. But there is so much more to Jesus than that. Where he came from, what he did on earth, what he can do for us now is all revealed in the Bible. This book contains the only record of Jesus and was written by the generation of people who heard him teach and saw his deeds. This is what the Bible teaches us about Jesus Christ:

We each come to this world with the divine Light of Christ inside us, with the innate ability to recognize truth about ourselves and about the Savior. Much like little children, Jesus Christ is deeply empathetic, so much so that He was capable of taking on the anguish and regret and pain of all of our sins. He suffered in the Garden of Gethsemane and on the cross under that immeasurable weight to ransom us from our mortal burdens. After three days He overcame death, emerging from the tomb resurrected and winning for us that same reward: he made possible our own resurrection, the permanent union of our spirit and perfected physical body. Jesus was sent by His Father to offer eternal life to all of His children; His sacrifice empowers the plan of salvation. Indeed, Christ asks us to be like little children, to reclaim the innate faith and unfeigned love of our early youth. Through the simplicity of loving Him, others, and ourselves as little children do, we can begin to understand the complexity of His life.

Jesus Christ was both divine and mortal, being the Only Begotten Son of God but also having a body of flesh and bone.

The Only Begotten Son was born to the virgin Mary, and He fulfilled ancient prophecies and covenants between God and His people. During Christ's ministry, He endowed priesthood and leadership authority upon many of His worthy followers on the earth and taught divine truths that were recorded in sacred scriptures. He administered saving temporal ordinances such as baptism, which he Himself submitted to though He had never sinned; the Savior did this because He asks us to follow Him in all things. He ministered to the sick and to the sinners with pure love and compassion. That compassion extends to each of us through the Atonement, a gift that satisfies the scales of justice by paying for our transgressions a gift only Jesus Christ could have given.

By humbling ourselves, repenting, and striving to keep His commandments, we can receive the blessings of the Savior's atoning sacrifice. Before His ministry began, Jesus Christ was a carpenter, and in many ways,

The activities of this first full year are mostly recorded in John 3-4. They begin in the spring of A.D. 27, when Jesus appeared in the temple at Passover and drove out the moneychangers, accusing them of making God's house "a house of merchandise." At the end of hisministry he cleared the temple again. Jesus apparently had done some miracles prior to this time,as Nicodemus came at night and said that no one could do such miracles if God were not with him. Nicodemus appears three times in John, ending as a disciple helping to bury his body.

After the Passover Jesus returned to Galilee, going through Samaria. There he met the Samaritan woman, leading to the conversion of her whole village. This account is in John; later the apostle John, along with Peter, was very interested in the spread of Christianity in Samaria

(Acts 8:14). When Jesus reached Galilee, he was rejected in Nazareth, and therefore moved from Nazareth to Capernaum, on the northern shore of the Lake of Galilee. Initially he stayed in Peter's home. Capernaum was to become his headquarters. Several of his closest disciples lived there.

The Synoptic Gospels record how Jesus selected his first disciples by the Lake of Galilee, as they were repairing their nets. They were two sets of brothers: James and John sons of Zebedee, and Peter and Andrew sons of Jonah. He told them to follow him and he would make them fishers of people. Actually, most of them had followed him for a while the previous year as recorded in John, but they had returned to their secular occupation. Now Jesus called them to follow him permanently; so they left their work and followed him, forsaking their parents and earthly means of support Matt 4:22; Luke 5:11. During the next months Jesus performed many miracles, especially healings, He still is. The carpenter considers a piece of wood's potential, examining its inherent strength, weakness, and grain, recognizing that what some people would see as unusable is actually an opportunity for singular beauty. Christ's skilled, patient hands can similarly transform us if we remain malleable and teachable, even as little children. In Matthew 18:4, Christ says, "Whosoever therefore shall humble himself as this little child, the same is greatest in the kingdom of heaven." When we become humble and rely on our Savior, we come to understand a great truth about ourselves: there is an inherent divinity the Light of Christ in each of us.

That light witnesses to the truthfulness of His gospel, which contains all of the covenants, principles, laws, ordinances, and doctrines we need to become more like our Heavenly Father and to return to Him.

The Death, Burial and Resurrection of Jesus the Messiah

The Gospel is a term that is used for a number of things in Christianity; it means good news essentially. The word is used for one or more of the four books of the Bible, Matthew, Mark, Luke, and John. These are the four gospels. But the word is also used very precisely for the central doctrines of the Christian faith concerning Jesus, namely his death, burial and resurrection. Paul clearly states that the Gospel that he preached is that Jesus died according to the Scriptures, was buried, and rose again according to the Scriptures. Paul says:

Now, brothers, I want to remind you of the gospel I preached to you, which you received and on which you have taken your stand. By this gospel you are saved, if you hold firmly to the word I preached to you. Otherwise, you have believed in vain. For what I received I passed on to you as of first importance: that Christ died for our sins according to the Scriptures, that he was buried, that he as raised on the third day according to the Scriptures 1 Cor. 15:1-4.

Paul then goes on to declare that Jesus made many appearances that proved that he did rise from the dead. And so the creed says: and was crucified also for us under Pontius Pilate; he suffered and was buried; and the third day he rose again according to the Scriptures.

The point is that the Christian Gospel is not simply the facts of Jesus' death, burial and resurrection, but those facts understood in accordance with what the Scriptures say. In other words, the death of Jesus has to be understood in accordance with what Scripture teaches about it who this Jesus was who died, why his death was so important, what kind of death it was, and what it accomplished. Likewise, the burial and the resurrection have to be understood in the way that Scripture teaches what exactly it teaches about his resurrection, why it was important, what it proved, and how it relates to his exaltation to glory. This would mean that we must first be clear on who Jesus is. If he is not God manifest in the flesh, if he is not the divine Son of God, then his death would be at best a martydom, a great act of love and devotion--but it would not have saved anyone, it would not have made atonement.

This would also mean that we would have to be clear on why he suffered and died. Scripture teaches that it was for our sins that he died (he did not deserve to die), the just for the unjust. His death was a vicarious substitutionary sacrifice for the sins of the world. And Scripture also teaches that his death was an atonement. In other words, it was not just a physical death. For the divine Son to die was the equivalent of the human race suffering the second death, eternal separation from God. Christ, the eternal one, was separated from the Father spiritually on our behalf when he died on the cross.

This would also mean that there was a complete death, and so he was buried. He did not swoon, or faint, or go into a coma to be revived. He died, and was buried. It was a real death.

And if it was a real death, this would also mean that it was a real resurrection, one who was dead actually coming back to life. The resurrection proved that his death was an atoning sacrifice, that it accomplished what it was accomplish, and that it authenticated all of Christ's claims.

It would take much longer to explain all the details about the Gospel that are contained in the Scripture. This is the task of the churches in their teaching and preaching ministry in the word of God. And we have our entire lifetime to focus on these truths and discover all that God has done for us. But perhaps it would be most helpful in this brief survey to look at the cardinal Old Testament prophecy about the death, burial and resurrection of the Messiah, Isaiah 52:15--53:12. The song is written in the past tense, as if it had alrready happened; but that is normal for the prophets who saw the visions and described what they had seen (called "seers"). We know from the contents of this song that its ultimate meaning is in Jesus the Messiah, for Jesus claimed to be the servant who came into the world to give his life a ransom for many Matt. 20:28, and the apostles knew that this song was a vivid picture of the suffering of the Lord Jesus on the cross and so quoted from it in their epistles see 1 Peter 2:21-25.

A Biblical Exposition Isaiah 52:15,53:12 is the fourth of the so-called Servant Songs in the book, and the most powerful of them all. The prophet Isaiah does not always identify the servant in the oracles; at times it seems it could be referring to the righteous remnant in Israel, at times to the prophet, at times to other servants that God might use. But in this passage, a song about the suffering servant, the meaning clearly breaks free from any Old Testament application and finds fulfillment in the Messiah, the Christ Jesus. Much of the song talks about how the innocent suffer for the sins of others, but when it comes to speaking about the LORD placing the sins of others on this one's back so that he could justify them, the passage can have no other fulfillment but in the saving death of Jesus, the Christ. And so this song is about the ideal suffering servant, the one whose suffering goes beyond anything that mere mortals could accomplish in their suffering.

Down through history the sufferer has been the astonishment and stumblingblock of humanity. Ancient barbarians simply removed them from society. More civilized people have dealt more kindly; but sufferers still pose a problem for philosophers and medical doctors, and a test for the faith of religious people. People have a hard time seeing any profit in suffering; rather, it is considered a tragedy, an inconvenience that hinders progress, a fate to be avoided.

Christ Our Healer ! Old Testament Verses Related to Healing

Psalm 103:2-5 Bless the LORD, O my soul, And forget not all His benefits: Who forgives all your iniquities, Who heals all your diseases, Who redeems your life from destruction, Who crowns you with loving kindness and tender mercies,Who satisfies your mouth with good things,So that your youth is renewed like the eagle's.

Jeremiah 17:14 Heal me, O LORD, and I shall be healed; Save me, and I shall be saved, For You are my praise. Jeremiah 30:17 For I will restore health to you And heal you of your wounds,' says the LORD, 'Because they called you an outcast saying:" This is Zion; No one seeks her."'

Hosea 6:1 Come, and let us return to the LORD; For He has torn, but He will heal us; He has stricken, but He will bind us up.

Hosea 14:4 I will heal their backsliding, I will love them freely, For My anger has turned away from him.

Malachi 4: But to you who fear My name The Sun of Righteousness shall arise With healing in His wings; And you shall go out And grow fat like stall-fed calves. Psalm 30:2-3 LORD my God, I cried out to You, And You healed me. O LORD, You brought my soul up from the grave; You have kept me alive, that I should not go down to the pit.

Exodus 15:26 and said, "If you diligently heed the voice of the LORD your God and do what is right in His sight, give ear to His commandments and keep all His statutes, I will put none of the diseases on you which I have brought on the Egyptians. For I am the LORD who heals you."

Deuteronomy 7:15 And the LORD will take away from you all sickness, and will afflict you with none of the terrible diseases of Egypt which you have known, but will lay them on all those who hate you.

Psalm 34:19 Many are the afflictions of the righteous, But the LORD delivers him out of them all.

Isaiah 53:4-5 Surely He has borne our griefs And carried our sorrows; Yet we esteemed Him stricken, Smitten by God, and afflicted. But He was wounded for our transgressions, He was bruised for our iniquities; The chastisement for our peace was upon Him, And by His stripes we are healed.

Jeremiah 33:6 Behold, I will bring it health and healing; I will heal them and reveal to them the abundance of peace and truth.

Isaiah 58:8 Then your light shall break forth like the morning, Your healing shall spring forth speedily, And your righteousness shall go before you; The glory of the LORD shall be your rear guard.

Psalm 41:3 The LORD will strengthen him on his bed of illness; You will sustain him on his sickbed.

Proverbs 3:7-8 Do not be wise in your own eyes; Fear the LORD and depart from evil. It will be health to your flesh, And strength to your bones.

Exodus 23:25 So you shall serve the LORD your God, and He will bless your bread and your water. And I will take sickness away from the midst of you.

Psalm 91:15-16 He shall call upon Me, and I will answer him; I will be with him in trouble; I will deliver him and honor him. With long life I will satisfy him, And show him My salvation.

Psalm 30:2 O LORD my God, I cried out to You, And You healed me.

Psalm 107:19-20 Then they cried out to the LORD in their trouble, And He saved them out of their distresses. He sent His word and healed them, And delivered them from their destruction.

Psalm 73:4-5 They have no struggles; their bodies are healthy and strong. They are free from the burdens common to man; they are not plagued by human ills.

Psalm 107:20 He sent forth his word and healed them; he rescued them from the grave.

Psalm 147:3 He heals the brokenhearted and binds up their wounds.

Isaiah 38:16 O Lord, by these things men live; And in all these things is the life of my spirit; So You will restore me and make me live.

Isaiah 57:18 I have seen his ways, and will heal him; I will also lead him, And restore comforts to him And to his mourners.

Jeremiah 33:6 Nevertheless, I will bring health and healing to it; I will heal my people and will let them enjoy abundant peace and security.

Psalm 34:19 Many are the afflictions of the righteous: but the Lord delivereth him out of them all.

Psalm 55:18 He hath delivered my soul in peace from the battle that was against me: for there were many with me.

Psalm 42:11 Why art thou cast down, O my soul? and why art thou disquieted within me? hope thou in God: for I shall yet praise him, who is the health of my countenance, and my God.

Psalm 25:17-18 The troubles of my heart are enlarged: O bring thou me out of my distresses. Look upon mine affliction and my pain; and forgive all my sins.

Job 4:3-4 Behold, thou hast instructed many, and thou hast strengthened the weak hands. [4] Thy words have upholden him that was falling, and thou hast strengthened the feeble knees.

Proverbs 16:24 Pleasant words are as an honeycomb, sweet to the soul, and health to the bones.

Psalm 6:2 Have mercy upon me, O Lord; for I am weak: O Lord, heal me; for my bones are vexed.

Psalm 27:14 Wait on the Lord: be of good courage, and he shall strengthen thine heart: wait, I say, on the Lord.

Psalm 28:7 The Lord is my strength and my shield; my heart trusted in him, and I am helped: therefore my heart greatly rejoiceth; and with my song will I praise him.

Psalm 31:24 Be of good courage, and he shall strengthen your heart, all ye that hope in the Lord.

Proverbs 17:22 A merry heart doeth good like a medicine: but a broken spirit drieth the bones.

Psalm 3:5 It laid me down and slept; I awaked; for the Lord sustained me.

Psalm 55:22 Cast thy burden upon the Lord, and he shall sustain thee: he shall never suffer the righteous to be moved.

Isaiah 40:29 He giveth power to the faint; and to them that have no might he increaseth strength.

New Testament Verses Related to Healing

Matthew 8:7 And Jesus said to him, I will come and heal him.

Matthew 4:23-24 And Jesus went about all Galilee, teaching in their synagogues, preaching the gospel of the kingdom, and healing all kinds of sickness and all kinds of disease among the people. 24 Then His fame went throughout all Syria; and they brought to Him all sick people who were afflicted with various diseases and torments, and those who were demon-possessed, epileptics, and paralytics; and He healed them all.

Matthew 8:5-8 Now when Jesus had entered Capernaum, a centurion came to Him, pleading with Him, saying, "Lord, my servant is lying at home paralyzed, dreadfully tormented." And Jesus said to him, "I will come and heal him." The centurion answered and said, "Lord, I am not worthy that You should come under my roof. But only speak a word, and my servant will be healed.

Matthew 8:17 That it might be fulfilled which was spoken by Esaias the prophet, saying, Himself took our infirmities, and bare our sicknesses.

Matthew 9:21-22 For she said to herself, If only I may touch His garment, I shall be made well. 22 But Jesus turned around, and when He saw her He said, Be of good cheer, daughter; your faith has made you well. And the woman was made well from that hour onwards.

Matthew 9:35 Then Jesus went about all the cities and villages, teaching in their synagogues, preaching the gospel of the kingdom, and healing every sickness and every disease among the people.

Matthew 15:28 Then Jesus answered and said to her, "O woman, great is your faith! Let it be to you as you desire." And her daughter was healed from that very hour.

Matthew 15:30 Then great multitudes came to Him, having with them the lame, blind, mute, maimed, and many others; and they laid them down at Jesus' feet, and He healed them.

Matthew 21:14 Then the blind and the lame came to Him in the temple, and He healed them.

Mark 16:17-18 And these signs will follow those who believe: In My name they will cast out demons; they will speak with new tongues; they will take up serpents; and if they drink anything deadly, it will by no means hurt them; they will lay hands on the sick, and they will recover."

Luke 4:40 When the sun was setting, all those who had any that were sick with various diseases brought them to Him; and He laid His hands on every one of them and healed them.

Luke 6:18 as well as those who were tormented with unclean spirits. And they were healed.

Luke 9:11 But when the multitudes knew it, they followed Him; and He received them and spoke to them about the kingdom of God, and healed those who had need of healing.

John 8:36 If the Son therefore shall make you free, ye shall be free indeed.

Acts 5:16 Also a multitude gathered from the surrounding cities to Jerusalem, bringing sick people and those who were tormented by unclean spirits, and they were all healed.

Romans 8:11 But if the Spirit of Him who raised Jesus from the dead dwells in you, He who raised Christ from the dead will also give life to your mortal bodies through His Spirit who dwells in you.

Romans 8:2 For the law of the Spirit of life in Christ Jesus hath made me free from the law of sin and death.

2 Corinthians 4:10-11 always carrying about in the body the dying of the Lord Jesus, that the life of Jesus also may be manifested in our body. 11 For we who live are always delivered to death for Jesus' sake, that the life of Jesus also may be manifested in our mortal flesh.

Philippians 4:7 And the peace of God, which passeth all understanding, shall keep your hearts and minds through Christ Jesus.

James 5:13-15 Is anyone among you suffering? Let him pray. Is anyone cheerful? Let him sing psalms. 14 Is anyone among you sick? Let him call for the elders of the church, and let them pray over him, anointing him with oil in the name of the Lord. 15 And the prayer of faith will save the sick, and the Lord will raise him up. And if he has committed sins, he will be forgiven.

1 Thessalonians 5:23 Now may the God of peace Himself sanctify you completely; and may your whole spirit, soul, and body be preserved blameless at the coming of our Lord Jesus Christ.

2 Timothy 1:7 For God hath not given us the spirit of fear; but of power, and of love, and of a sound mind.

1 Peter 2:24 who Himself bore our sins in His own body on the tree, that we, having died to sins, might live for righteousness-by whose stripes you were healed. 3 John 1:2 Beloved, I pray that you may prosper in all things and be in health, just as your soul prospers.

God, being our Father, wants to heal us much more than we want to be healed. Jesus wants to heal us so much He decided to be wounded, and by His wounds we are healed 1 Pt 2:24. The Holy Spirit wants to heal us much more than we can imagine, for our bodies are temples of the Spirit 1 Cor 6:19. If God the Father, Son, and Holy Spirit want to heal us so much, then why are so many people not healed?

Many Christians have patterned their healing ministries after imperfect copies of imperfect copies of Jesus' healing ministry, and thus have deviated more and more from the original. Possibly because of these deviations, we do not get Jesus' results, that is, immediate physical healings of all those He tried to heal. We may need to un-learn much of what we have carelessly imitated, and then learn carefully what the Bible reveals about Jesus' healing ministry. All healing ministries must be based on God's word and not on spiritual experiences or psychological theories.

Healing In God's Plan

When anyone begin any ministry, they should first seek God's vision for the ministry because "without vision, the people perish" (Prv 29:18, KJV). We must see the big picture to know how we fit in. The following seven truths are part of the Father's plan for the healing ministry:

1. Healing is to accompany the proclamation of God's word and lead people to accept Jesus as Lord and Savior (Mk 16:17-18). What shall it profit a man to gain perfect physical health, but lose his soul? see Lk 9:25 What good is it to be the healthiest person in hell? One of the Greek words for healing means salvation. Jeremiah prays:

Heal me, Lord, that I may be healed; save me, that I may be saved Jer 17:14.

2. Healing is a sign of God's kingdom (Matthew 10:7-8). It rallies, restores and empowers believers to build the kingdom.

3. Our heavenly Father loves His children and wants them healed. His principal motivation for healing is love.

4. Healers are to raise up and disciple other healers. The Lord wants hundreds of millions of people in this ministry.

5. Jesus heals the whole person. He wants us healed in every way physically, mentally, psychologically, sexually and spiritually.

6. Jesus heals by families (see Ex 20:5-6). He not only sees us as individuals but as community. "If one member suffers, all the members suffer with it" (1 Cor 12:26).

7. God the Father has authorized only one healing ministry, that of His Son. Jesus continues to heal today through us, His body. "Jesus Christ is the same yesterday, today, and forever" (Heb 13:8). We should not start our own healing ministry but join the healing ministry of Jesus.

The Imitation Of Christ As Healer

Because Jesus has the only legitimate healing ministry, we equip Christians to heal by teaching them to imitate Christ. Jesus equipped the apostles to heal by taking them on tour with Him. They saw Him healing in many circumstances see Mt, Chapters 8 and 9. Then Jesus sent them out with authority to heal as He healed Mt 10:1. They simply imitated Jesus. For example, when Peter raised Tabitha Dorcas from the dead Acts 9:40, he made the mourners leave the room where the body was, just as Jesus had done when He raised the daughter of Jairus Mk 5:40. Then Peter commanded Tabitha to get up; Jesus said Talitha, get up. Peter only had to change the. Healing is the imitation of Christ.

An amazing thing about Jesus' healing ministry is that in the Gospels we never see Him praying for the sick. In James 5:14, we are called to pray for the sick, but we have no record of Jesus ever praying for the sick. He almost always healed by giving a command. The statement of the centurion is the essence of Jesus' healing ministry: I am not worthy to have You under my roof. Just give an order and my boy will get better see Mt 8:8. Jesus heals by giving doctor's orders see Mk 2:17. He heals by being Lord. Jesus is Lord first and foremost, and He is Healer, Teacher, Prophet, Pastor, etc. only insofar as it manifests His lordship. Jesus was unique "because He taught with authority, and not like the scribes Mk 1:22. Jesus usually commanded the sick person to do something. At other times He commanded the devil to leave. He even ordered a fever to leave Simon's mother-in-law Lk 4:39.

Jesus was able to heal by exercising His authority because He knew whom to command and what to command. He knew when the sick person needed a deeper faith in Him and how to help the sick person grow in faith. He knew whether unforgiveness or other sins were the causes of the sickness and whether the devil was involved in the sickness. Jesus rose early every morning to listen to His Father Mk 1:35, and He prayed into the night on many occasions Lk 22:39. Jesus did not pray for healing but before healing. He did nothing and said nothing except what the Father told Him Jn 5:19; 8:28. Jesus gave us authority over all demons and every disease Mt 10:1, but we can't be in authority unless we are under authority to our heavenly Father. This implies that we take time to hear Him and then obey Him and give commands for healing.

Do I Have The Gift Of Healing? Even when we know how to heal as Jesus did, we must know if we are called to the healing ministry. All Christians can heal by their faith in Jesus Christ see Mk 16:18, but not all are equally gifted healers 1 Cor 12:30. For example, almost all human beings can run, sing, or think, but some are especially gifted in these ways. In my experience, I find that about one-third of Christians are especially gifted healers, but very few know this. They rarely, if ever, use their healing gift while countless sick people go through these healers' lives without receiving healing. In a world of sickness and pain, this is a sad waste of supernatural resources.

How do we know if we have a special gift of healing? The Spirit reveals this to us through prayer, the Bible, our brothers and sisters in Christian community, and especially through the events of everyday life. It is easy to find out the extent of our gift of healing. For example, how can we tell whether we have the gift of running? If we just run for a while, it will become obvious. Likewise, if we minister healing to a couple hundred people over a few months, we will know by the fruits if we have a special gift of healing see Mt 7:20.

Although God made it simple to see the extent of our healing gift, we complicate matters by pride, self-hatred, and confusion. In some groups, a healing ministry is well-respected, and some will wrongly seek it because of pride. Others have the mistaken idea that they need to be worthy and thereby automatically disqualify themselves from using any of God's gifts, including healing. Still others say the Lord chooses the healed to be the healers 2 Cor 1:4. There is some truth to this, but the main way to tell if we have a special gift of healing is simply to observe over a period of time if people are healed.

The Identity And Character Of A Healer

When we are under the lordship of Jesus and open to the Spirit, we can know who we are in Christ. If we think we may have the gift of healing in a special way, we should ask the Holy Spirit to confirm this 2 Cor 1:21. If we don't let the Spirit make us very aware of our healing ministry, we will miss over 90 percent of our opportunities to heal, probably become discouraged, and may even quit when the devil comes against our ministry.

After our identity as healers is confirmed by the Spirit, we have the basis for developing the Christian character of a healer. Often those in a healing ministry are immature in their relationship with the Lord Mth 7:22. They just ride the wave of healing's excitement for a while but disdain the discipline of the Lord Heb 12:5. If our healing ministry is to last and bear abundant fruit, we must mature in Christian character and develop a life-style that will protect and nurture our healing ministry. We need a new wineskin for the new wine of healing Lk 5:37. Otherwise, the new wine of healing will be wasted and our lives will be disrupted. We need to develop Christian character for the healing ministry in the following ways:

1. Those in a healing ministry need to spend at least an hour or more daily in prayer. Much of this prayer should be scheduled for a regular

time each day. Remember Jesus prayed before healing rather than for healing.

2. Those in a healing ministry should go to Confession the Sacrament of Reconciliation at least monthly. In God's service, we can expect persecution and spiritual warfare 2 Tm 3:12. It is disastrous to give the devil an opening by not repenting of sin and not being reconciled to the Church.

3. A healer's life should be in God's order. We should be in Christian community, under the authority of the Church, and accountable to a pastor. The marriages and families of those in healing ministry should be ordered according to Biblical principles Ephesians, Chapters 5 and 6.

4. A healer needs a simple life-style so that the cares of the world will not choke the movement of the Spirit Mk 4:18-19. "My point is that you should live in accord with the Spirit and you will not yield to the cravings of the flesh. The flesh lusts against the Spirit and the Spirit against the flesh; the two are directly opposed" Gal 5:16-17. A worldly life-style may ruin more healing ministries than any other cause.

5. The Lord will often bestow on members of a healing ministry a special love for the sick. We should pray often throughout the day for this love, because our healing ministry will not be beneficial without such a love 1 Cor 13:1-3.

Healing By Obeying Jesus' Commands

Because the Lord loves us so much, He usually doesn't want only to heal us, but also to do several other things for us. Therefore, healing is usually part of a "package" including such other things as conversion, forgiveness, repentance, evangelization, vocation, ministry, or more. The Lord may give us a whole series of commands that touch many areas of our lives. All of these areas are intertwined with our healing. Consequently, to accept healing, there are usually several areas in which we must obey the Lord. If we have persisted in rebellion and sin in these areas of our lives even to the point of blinding ourselves to God's will, then obedience becomes difficult. For this reason we may wish that the Lord hadn't mixed healing in with so many other things. We find the Lord "too much for us" Mk 6:3, but we can accept God's grace to be healed of spiritual blindness. Then we will repent, obey the Lord's commands, be healed, and give healing by giving the Lord's commands.

Isa 58:6-11 Is not this the fast that I have chosen? to loose the bands of wickedness, to undo the heavy burdens, and to let the oppressed go free, and that ye break every yoke? Is it not to deal thy bread to the hungry, and that thou bring the poor that are cast out to thy house? when thou seest the naked, that thou cover him; and that thou hide not thyself from thine own flesh? 8 Then shall thy light break forth as the morning, and thine health shall spring forth speedily: and thy righteousness shall go before thee; the glory of the LORD shall be thy rereward. 9 Then shalt thou call, and the LORD shall answer; thou shalt cry, and he shall say, Here I am. If thou take away from the midst of thee the yoke, the putting forth of the finger, and speaking vanity; 10 And if thou draw out thy soul to the hungry, and satisfy the afflicted soul; then shall thy light rise in obscurity, and thy darkness be as the noonday: 11 And the LORD shall guide thee continually, and satisfy thy soul in drought, and make fat thy bones: and thou shalt be like a watered garden, and like a spring of water, whose waters fail not.

The affirmations behavior change Bible and Health Christian eternal life Exercise faith Faith and Health fitness food forgiveness Freedom God Healing Health health care heart Holy Spirit hope Jesus joy Life love mind body spirit obedience obesity peace power prayer relationships running scripture sin spiritual exercises Spiritual Fitness spirituality and health strength stress the research thinking trust Twitter weight loss wellness wholeness

.But for the Christian the point of suffering should be clearer. In summary, we may say that the Scriptures teach that it is the will of God that believers suffer--not all the time, not all the same, and some very little. That is not to say that God enjoys it, or that people should seek it. But the Bible says that it is inevitable. Jesus said that if the world hated him, it would hate us as well. Paul said all who live Godly lives in this world will suffer persecution (2 Tim. 3), and that it was given to us to believe and to suffer (Phil. 1:29). And Peter explains that Christ's death, revealed so fully in Isaiah, is both our justification and our sample to follow so that we might know how to suffer (1 Pet. 2:19-23). Moreover, our Lord himself learned obedience through the things that he suffered (Heb. 5:8)--and if that is true of the sinless Son of God, how much more is it true of us? All of these teachings simply say that suffering is inevitable in this life, especially if we seek to live a righteous life of spiritual service.

The sample for us to follow in our suffering--if it comes--is the suffering of Jesus Christ our Lord. It is displayed graphically in the prophecy of Isaiah, written centuries before the actual death of Jesus. Isaiah displays the ideal sufferer, but never names him. That identification had to await the fulness of time, when Jesus claimed, and the disciples could see, that Jesus was fulfilling Isaiahs oracles.

The word gospel literally means "good news," and how could the gospel of Jesus Christ be otherwise? The fundamental gospel elements are these: faith in Jesus Christ, repentance, baptism, receiving the gift of the Holy Spirit, and enduring to the end. Throughout the history of humankind, the gospel has been preached by God's prophets. In 1830 Jesus Christ restored His gospel for our day through a prophet named Joseph Smith. The Lord instructed Joseph Smith to bring forth and translate the ancient scriptural text known as the Book of Mormon. The Savior also restored the keys of the priesthood and the saving ordinances that are required for His Church to accomplish His work again on earth. The Prophet Joseph Smith received revelation from God, as have all his successors, and during their lives they have all taught the gospel of Jesus Christ to the people of their time. The current prophet does so today. From each of these prophets we learn what is required of us to become more like God and to prepare to live with Him again.

There are five fundamentals of Christ's gospel. The first is faith in Jesus Christ. It isn't enough to believe in Christ; we also have to believe Him—believe that we can be made whole through His Atonement and that we are worthy of such a gift. Through faith, our minds and hearts are opened, and the words of the gospel find room to settle in and imprint on us. Such faith and humility brings about the second gospel step: repentance. We want to correlate our actions with our beliefs, to align our behavior with our thoughts, so not only do we seek sincere forgiveness for previous misdeeds, but we also actively turn toward Christ and a new way of living our lives.

This commitment to a "new normal" way of living is demonstrated through the act of baptism by immersion, the third step in our progression.

Baptism is a symbolic ordinance of cleansing that signifies our rebirth as disciples of Christ and followers of His gospel. We join His Church and make sacred covenants to God. As the fourth step along our path, we then receive the gift of the Holy Ghost, and our sins are forgiven. As a member of the Godhead, the Holy Ghost is one with God and Jesus Christ in character and in purpose. He is the conduit of Their love and knowledge, and He is given to us as a constant companion if we remain worthy. He speaks to us in a "still, small voice" to communicate to us the will of God and provide guidance and direction. As the Apostles of Christ did when they were on the earth, priesthood holders today place their hands on the heads of the newly baptized and confer the Holy Spirit upon them.

While the ordinances of baptism and receiving the gift of the Holy Ghost may seem almost momentary in their brevity, the process of following the gospel itself is one of enduring commitment, a promise we make to retain the freshness of conversion always and to constantly recommit ourselves. Enduring to the end is the fifth step in this journey that eventually leads to salvation. Taking the sacrament weekly is an important part of this process, and each time we partake of the bread and water, we remember Jesus Christ and His Atonement and we remember to keep the commandments of the restored gospel.

Jesus Christ leads His restored Church today, and indeed, the Church bears His name: it is The Church of Jesus Christ of Latter-day Saints.

He is assisted by earthly Apostles now as He was during His ministry. The Book of Mormon, which was kept and preserved to be brought forth in our day, is another witness of Jesus Christ. It includes teachings of the Savior and clarifies many aspects of the gospel. It also tells of His visit to the Americas, where He taught the people there as He had done in Israel; this is another witness that the Savior's message is for everyone. Today, around the world, some 80,000 young Mormon missionaries are bringing this testament of Him to all who will reclaim the teachability of their youth, allowing the book's truth about our Redeemer and about the inherent divinity of each of us to be confirmed by the Light of Christ inside them. That light is in us; it is in others; it is part of what binds us together as a people as His people.

Millions of people know about Jesus Christ. But fewer claim to actually know Him as a divine being, as the Savior, as our brother. Is it enough to know who Jesus is and His role in our Heavenly Father's plan? That knowledge is really only the beginning.

Beginning before the Nativity and extending through the Crucifixion and Resurrection, JESUS OF NAZARETH brings to life all the sweeping drama in the life of Jesus, as told by the Gospels.

Luke 23:28 But Jesus turning to them said, Daughters of Jerusalem, weep not John 20:13 and they say to her, Woman, why weep you? She said to them,

Genesis 49:9, 10 Judah is a lion's whelp: from the prey, my son, you are gone up:

Numbers 24:9 He couched, he lay down as a lion, and as a great lion: who shall

Hebrews 7:14 for it is evident that our Lord sprang out of Judah; of which tribe

" the last week of Christ, but it is so intense. I have to give "Jesus of Nazareth" the highest rating possible

The phrase "Lamb of God" is a reference to the Passover lamb whose shed blood saved God's people from death and freed them from their bondage to slavery in Egypt (Exodus 12:12-13).

THE LION OF JUDAH

Paul called Jesus our "Passover Lamb" in 1 Cor. 5:7, and John the Baptist introduced Jesus as "the Lamb of God who takes away the sin of the world" (John 1:29). He was saying that as the Passover lamb redeemed the Jews from their bondage to slavery, the Lamb of God redeems us from our bondage to sin.

Lion of Judah comes from Genesis 49:9-12 where Jacob called his son Judah a lion's cub, and prophesied that the Messiah would come from the tribe of Judah and be the ruler over the nations. That makes "Lion of Judah" a Messianic title and since Jesus is the Messiah who will rule the world, He is the Lion of Judah.

Therefore The "Lamb of God" is a title associated with the Lord's first Coming, while the "Lion of Judah" points to His second coming.

Jesus Of Nazareth

The many notable qualities of the lion are often applied figuratively in a variety of ways to individuals and nations. The king is frightening in his anger (Prov 19:12; 20:2), the soldier courageous (2 Sam 17:10), national leaders vicious (Ezek 22:25; Zeph 3:3), enemy nations destructive (Isa 5:29; Jer 2:15) and protective of their conquests (Isa 5:29), and personal enemies stealthy in their pursuit to harm (Psalm 10:9; 17:12).

God is described with a number of leonine features. He is strong (Isa 38:13), fearless in protecting his own (Isa 31:4), stealthy in coming upon his prey (Jer 49:19; Hosea 13:7), frightening (Hosea 11:10; Amos 3:8), and destructive (Jer 25:38; Lam 3:10; Hosea 5:14; 13:8). In am 3:8 "The Lion" even appears as a title for God.

The idea of a Lion of the Tribe of Judah is problematic because the fundamental passage (Rev 5:5) is grammatically ambiguous and because there is no exact antecedent parallel. First, it is unclear whether in Revelation 5:5 we have one title of Christ (Lion of the Tribe of Judah) or two titles standing in apposition (The Lion; The One of the Tribe of Judah). Second, the alleged parallels are only approximate parallels. In Genesis 49:9 there is no lion of Judah; rather, Judah is a lion. In 2 (4) Esdras 11:37; 12:1, 31 the Messiah is pictured as a lion, but not specifically of Judah. In the Testament of Judah 24:5 the Messiah is from Judah but not specifically as a lion. Given the imprecision in the alleged parallels, the cautious interpreter would not make much of the tradition that combines "lion" and "of the Tribe of Judah" into one idea, but rather would understand Jesus the Lamb to be called Messiah under two images derived from separate traditions.

Finally, the lion figure is expansive enough in its manifold facets to suggest its application to Satan. Such meaning is possible in 2 Timothy 4:17, but 1pe 5:8 is its classic occurrence. Here Satan is portrayed as both frightening his prey and silently stalking it to devour it. This devouring is best seen as potentially successful and as consisting of physical death. Therefore, professing believers should not lose faith, even in the face of the devil's most relentless pressures to give up.

THE LION OF JUDAH

The lion is not found in Palestine at the present day, though in ancient times it is known to have inhabited not only Syria and Palestine but also Asia Minor and the Balkan Peninsula, and its fossil remains show that it was contemporary with prehistoric man in Northwestern Europe and Great Britain. Its present range extends throughout Africa, and it is also found in Mesopotamia, Southern Persia, and the border of India. There is some reason to think that it may be found in Arabia, but its occurrence there remains to be proved. The Asiatic male lion does not usually have as large a mane as the African, but both belong to one species,

"How should we understand the Lion and the Lamb passage?"

Answer: Typically, when someone is thinking of the "lion and the lamb," Isaiah 11:6 is in mind due to it often being misquoted, "And the wolf will dwell with the lamb, and the leopard will lie down with the young goat, and the calf and the young lion and the fatling together." The true "Lion and the Lamb" passage is Revelation 5:5–6. The Lion and the Lamb both refer to Jesus Christ. He is both the conquering Lion of the tribe of Judah and the Lamb who was slain. The Lion and the Lamb are descriptions of two aspects of the nature of Christ. As the Lion of Judah, He fulfils the prophecy of Genesis 49:9 and is the Messiah who would come from the tribe of Judah. As the Lamb of God, He is the perfect and ultimate sacrifice for sin.

The scene of Revelation 4—5 is the heavenly throne room. After receiving the command to write to the seven churches in Asia Minor, John is "caught up in the spirit" to the throne room in heaven where he is to receive a series of visions that culminate in the ultimate victory of Christ at the end of the age. Revelation 4 shows us the endless praise that God receives from the angels and the 24 elders. Chapter 5 begins with John noticing that there is a scroll in the "right hand of him who was seated on the throne." The scroll has writing on the inside and is sealed with seven seals.

After giving us a description of the scroll, an angel proclaims with a loud voice, "Who is worthy to open the scroll and break its seals?" John begins to despair when no one comes forth to answer the angel's challenge. One of the 24 elders encourages John to "weep no more," and points out that the Lion of the tribe of Judah has come to take and open the scroll. The Lion of the tribe of Judah is obviously a reference to Christ. The image of the lion is meant to convey kingship. Jesus is worthy to receive and open the scroll because he is the King of God's people.

Back in Genesis 49:9, when Jacob was blessing his sons, Judah is referred to as a "lion's cub," and in verse 10 we learn that the "sceptre shall not depart from Judah." The scepter is a symbol of lordship and power. This was a prophecy that in Israel the kingly line would be descended from Judah. That prophecy was fulfilled when David succeeded to the throne after the death of King Saul (2 Samuel). David was descended from the line of Judah, and his descendants were the kings in Israel/Judah until the time of the Babylonian captivity in 586 BC.

This imagery of kingship is further enhanced when Jesus is described as the "root of David." This harkens us back to the words of Isaiah the prophet: "There shall come forth a shoot from the stump of Jesse, and a branch from his roots shall bear fruit. . . . In that day the root of Jesse, who shall stand as a signal for the peoples of him shall the nations inquire, and his resting place shall be glorious" (Isaiah 11:1, 10). As the root of David, Jesus is not only being identified as a descendant of David, but also the source or "root" of David's kingly power.

Why is Jesus worthy to open the scroll? He is worthy because He "has conquered." We know that, when Jesus returns, He will conquer all of God's enemies, as graphically described in Revelation 19. However, more importantly, Jesus is worthy because He has conquered sin and death at the cross. The cross was the ultimate victory of God over the forces of sin and evil. The events that occur at the return of Christ are the "mop-up" job to finish what was started at the cross. Because Jesus secured the ultimate victory at Calvary, He is worthy to receive and open the scroll, which contains the righteous judgment of God.

Christ's victory at the cross is symbolized by his appearance as a "Lamb standing, as though it had been slain" (Revelation 5:6). Prior to the exodus from Egypt, the Israelites were commanded by God to take an unblemished lamb, slay it, and smear its blood on the doorposts of their homes (Exodus 12:1–7). The blood of the slain lamb would set apart the people of Israel from the people of Egypt when the death angel came during the night to slay the firstborn of the land. Those who had the blood of the lamb would be spared. Fast forward to the days of John the Baptist. When he sees Jesus approaching him, he declares to all present, "Behold, the Lamb of God, who takes away the sin of the world!" (John 1:29). Jesus is the ultimate "Passover lamb" who saves His people from eternal death.

So when Jesus is referred to as the Lion and the Lamb, we are to see Him as not only the conquering King who will slay the enemies of God at His return, but also as the sacrificial Lamb who took away the reproach of sin from His people so they may share in His ultimate victory.

The Gospel of Matthew

Why Are There Four Gospels?

The first thing to notice about the Gospels is that they are skilfully designed; each one is tailored to suit its specific perspective. Matthew was a Jew, a Levite; he presents Jesus Christ as the Messiah of Israel "the Lion of the Tribe of Judah. This first book of the New Testament plunges right in to establish Jesus as the Meshach Nagged, the Messiah the King.

After first establishing the royal genealogy, Matthew then proceeds to focus on the fulfilment of the Old Testament prophecies: Matthew uses the term fulfilled 82 times! Again, his interest was to present

Jesus as the Messiah of Israel; Jesus credentials are that He fulfilled prophecy.

The first miracle described in Matthew is also very Jewish "the leper was cleansed, and leprosy was, to Jews, a sign of sin. Matthew also ended his Gospel in a very Jewish way; with the Resurrection. Matthew left out the Ascension, but remembers that it is not a milestone in respect to Jesus Messianic mission His return, however, will be.

Stenographic Skill

Matthew emphasized what Jesus said. He evidently recorded the discourses verbatim. As a customs official, he was a tachygraphy, or shorthand writer.1 the reason Matthews Gospel is so much longer than Marks is that he includes Jesus extensive discourses, such as the Sermon on the Mount and the Olivet Discourse; without these discourses, Marks Gospel is longer!

Many scholars now believe that the Gospels were written before Pauls first imprisonment in 57-60 A.D., and that virtually all of the New Testament books were written before Jerusalem's destruction.

There is no hint in the New Testament of Nero's persecutions after 64 A.D., nor of the execution of James, the Lords brother, in 62 A.D. There is not the slightest mention of the Jewish revolt against the Romans, which began in 66 A.D., or of the destruction of Jerusalem in 70 A.D. These historic events would have been irresistible in making many of the arguments in the New Testament documents.

In Revelation 5, John weeps bitterly or convulsively for no one is found worthy to open the scroll. The passages are clear that nobody in Heaven, neither on Earth, nor under the Earth was or is worthy. Where then was Jesus before He appeared and took the scroll? John seems to indicate that the Lamb appeared freshly slain. So was John taken back to crucifixion? It seems while Jesus was on the cross bearing sin, He wouldn't be technically worthy. Or was John in the future, and at the time John was weeping Jesus was in transit to the Father and was not found at that particular moment.

A. I don't see anything in Rev. 5:6 that requires the Lord to have been freshly slain. The literal translation speaks of a Lamb "as it had been slain". The words "had been" are in the past perfect tense indicating the act of slaying Him took place in the past and was over. Many scholars interpret the phrase "Lamb as it had been slain" as meaning the Lord will still be in human form and will bear the scars of His ordeal.

And you're correct in saying that He wasn't really "worthy" until after the resurrection when His act of redemption was proven to be complete. I don't think the verses leading up to Rev. 5:6 are intended to imply that Jesus is not present. I think they serve the purpose of confirming that in all of creation Jesus is the only one who can open the scroll and begin the end time's judgments that will culminate in His return as King of the whole Earth Zechariah 14:9.

The scroll John saw was in God's right hand, with writing on both sides Revelation chapter 5:1a. Being in His right hand indicates His authority and power. Whatever is in the scroll has been designed, planned, and will be executed from the will of ADONAI. It originated from His right hand. This scroll contains the title deed to the earth, which will be given to God the Son. Unlike other deeds, it will not give the details of what Jesus will inherit, but rather how He will regain His rightful inheritance. He will do so by means of His wrath poured out on the earth. But the scroll will not only judge those on the earth, it will also redeem, or buy the earth back from Satan, his demons and his followers. Later in the book John will symbolically eat this scroll. And when he eats it, it turns as sweet as honey to his taste, but it will turn his stomach sour Revelation 10:9-10. It tastes sweet because John wants Jesus to act in judgment and take back the earth that is rightfully His. But the realization of the terrible doom awaiting unbelievers turned that initial sweet taste into bitterness. Something similar happened in the book of Ezekiel. In his vision of heaven, Ezekiel said: I looked, and I saw a hand stretched out to me. In it was a scroll, which God unrolled before me. Normally, scrolls were written only on one side. But like John's scroll, this scroll was written on both sides, and it contained words of lament and mourning and woe. And God said to Ezekiel, "Son of man eat this scroll; then go back and speak to the house of Israel. So I opened my mouth, and he gave me the scroll to eat. And it became as sweet as honey in my mouth Ezekiel 2:9 to 3:3. The implication of it being written on both sides is that it points to the importance and the terrible nature of the events that are being recorded.

The book of Zechariah also gives us some insight as to why the terrible events of the Great Tribulation will take place Zechariah 5:1-4. He also saw a scroll, a very large flying scroll, and like the two tablets of the Testimony Exodus 32:15, it was written on both sides. And God said to Zechariah, "This is the curse that is going out over the whole world; for according to what it says on one side, every thief will be banished." This refers to one of the first four commandments. "And according to what it says on the other, everyone who swears falsely will be banished," and this refers to one of the last six of the Ten Commandments. The curse of the scroll is directed against those who violate one of the commandments on each side of the two tablets – the eighth commandment against stealing on the back Exodus 20:15 and the third commandment against swearing falsely by misusing the name of the LORD on the front (Exodus 20:7).162 The point is, the terrible events of the Great Tribulation will happen because of a total violation of God's moral standards that are revealed in the scroll, beautifully displayed in Christ and constantly taught in the word.

This scroll was sealed with seven steals 5:1b. Sealing a scroll was a common and important practice in Biblical times. The wills of both Emperor Vespasian and Cesar Augustus, for example, were secured with seven seals. For such a document, a scribe would procure a long roll of parchment and begin writing. After a period of writing he would stop, roll the parchment just enough to cover his words.

Then he would seal the scroll at that point with wax. Then he would resume writing, stop again, roll the scroll, and add another seal. By the time he was finished, he would have sealed the scroll seven times. Then the scroll is like a will, and would be read a section at a time, after each seal was opened. The only one, who could break the seals, was the one who would receive the inheritance after the death of the testator, or the one who made the will. In case, the Messiah is both the testator and the one who will receive the inheritance.

Jeremiah 32:9-15 gives us a good picture of such a scroll. In the last days of the southern kingdom of Judah, just before the fall of Jerusalem, Jeremiah's cousin Hanamel needed help. He was desperate to sell a field he owned in Jeremiah's hometown of Anathoth, near Jerusalem. The Babylonian army was coming into the Land like a flood and once they conquered Judah, Hanamel's field would be worthless. But contrary to human wisdom, and in obedience to God's command, Jeremiah bought his cousins field and put the sealed copy of the scroll in a clay jar so it would last a long time as a sign that the exile in Babylon would not last forever see my commentary on Jeremiah, Jeremiah Buys a Field.

Who had the power to defeat the Devil and his demons, to do away with sin and to reverse the curse on all the earth? And John saw a mighty angel, Gabriel himself, shouting in loud voice, "Who is worthy to break the seals and open the scroll?" In answer to Gabriel's question there is only silence since the angel is not named in Scripture, it may be Gabriel because his name denotes mighty. The angels of heaven wait in silence. Noah, Abraham, Isaac, Jacob, Job, Moses, David, Isaiah, Jeremiah, Daniel, the apostles and everyone from the Church Age all stand in silence. After scouring every level of the universe, it seems like no one in heaven God's holy angels or on earth all of humanity or under the earth Satan and all of his fallen angels could open the scroll, even look inside it 5:2-3.

Overwhelmed with grief and sadness John wept and wept, literally kept on shedding many tears, because no one was found who was worthy to open the scroll or look inside it Revelation 5:4. Wept is from klaio, and is the same word used to describe Jesus' weeping over Jerusalem Luke 19:41, and Peter's bitter weeping after betraying Christ three times Luke 22:62. It is a word that expresses uncontrollable sobbing and heaving. John was broken hearted because unless that book can be opened there is no hope. There is only one hope for this world, the glorious appearing of our great God and Saviour, Yeshua the Messiah. He is the blessed hope Titus 2:13. No one can help us but Jesus.

Interestingly enough, this is the only time we see tears in heaven. John's tears represent the tears of God's people throughout the ages. Those tears represent your tears and my tears as we experience the trials, the sufferings, the heartaches and indescribable disappointments of this life. Sometimes the pain is so great we don't know if we can go on. But the good news is that one day God promises to wipe away every tear from our eyes Revelation 7:17, 21:4. In the midst of our pain, sometimes that promise is hard to imagine, but we continue to hope in Him Job 13:15. That is why we wait for the blessed hope.

But ADONAI's mercy and grace would never allow the world to drown in a sea of hopelessness. In the midst of our despair, Jesus was about to take action. One of the twenty-four elders told John not to weep. Why was it necessary for one of the elders to comfort John, who already knew that Jesus had triumphed? Because John did that which we so easily do, he lost sight of the victory of the Lamb, which always results in hopelessness and tears. How very often do we sadden Jesus with our weeping and discouragement? We are often ready to give up in spite of the fact that He has already achieved the final victory.

Then John's attention was drawn to a new Person emerging at the throne of God. No human or angel can buy back the universe. But there is One who can. He is our great God and Saviour Jesus Christ and here he is identified by the first of His two messianic titles. The elder said: See, the Lion of the Tribe of Judah, the Root of David, has

THE LION OF JUDAH

triumphed Revelation 5:5a. The title the Lion of the Tribe of Judah comes from Jacob's blessing. When Jacob was dying, he called his twelve sons around him, and prophesied to Leah's fourth born: You are a lion's cub, O Judah the scepter or the right to rule will not depart from Judah until He comes to whom it belongs and the obedience of the nations is His Genesis 49:9-10. In John's day the Romans had destroyed Jerusalem, the heart of Judah, and the Jews were scattered throughout the world. The scepter had indeed departed from Judah, and the One to whom it belonged had already come, been rejected and crucified. The Lord Jesus is the Lion of the Tribe of Judah, but he is also the Root of David Isaiah 11:1 and 10. Yeshua the Messiah is in absolute control.

The title the Root, or descendant, of David comes from a prophecy in Second Samuel 7:5-16, the great chapter of God's covenant with David, where ADONAI said: Your house and your kingdom will last forever before me; your throne will be established forever. At that time ADONAI promised King David that one of his descendants would be the Messiah. Yeshua fulfilled that prophecy. Jesus' earthly mother was Mary, a descendant of David see my commentary on The Life of Christ. The Genealogies of Joseph and Mary Thus, Messiah has the right to rule because He is the fulfilment of the prophecies made in the Holy Scriptures. All of those prophecies will be fulfilled at Christ's Second Coming when He establishes His millennial Kingdom.

Yeshua will be the only one worthy to open the scroll because He has triumphed. The scroll or the will was written in the name of Christ, since it is His inheritance. He is also the One who died, and because of the resurrection, thus He is the only one worthy to open His own scroll or will. It is the most unusual will ever written because all of the inheritance goes to the one whom

Died! In the Greek this word is in the aorist active tense and points to a once for all-time victory. At the cross He triumphed over sin Romans 8:3, death Hebrews 2:14-15, and the forces of hell Colossians 2:15; First Peter 3:19. For everyone born of God overcomes the world First

John 5:4 because He has triumphed. John stopped sobbing long enough to see the Lion prepare to open the scroll and its seven steals Revelation 5:5b. What excitement there will be as all of heaven holds its collective breath, waiting for Yeshua to tear off the seals, open the scroll and take back what is rightfully His.

John was writing to first-century believers who were suffering greatly under persecution. Many had lost all their possessions and were being threatened with death if they did not renounce the Lord. The evil that confronted them seemed so vast that they undoubtedly were tempted to think that darkness would triumph.

We too can be tempted in this way when we are engulfed in suffering – whether it is because of disease, life's problems, moral sufferings, or the sinful state of our society. John may well have written to strengthen and encourage the believers of his age, but his words can speak to us also, giving us a firm foundation for our security and assurance. ADONAI is on our side. God the Son has triumphed over evil and has already paid for every sin you will ever commit past, present or future. That's why faith is so important. There is no hope except what Christ has already done. You need to believe in what Yeshua has already done for you, not believing what you can do for Him.

In his vision, John saw Jesus prepared to regain His rightful inheritance. Such a vision and the truths that such a vision reveals can give us great comfort and security. Every one of God's intentions toward us is for our good, not for evil. Every thought He has for us had to do with our blessing, our prosperity, and our growth in His holiness. At one time, it looked as if no one could open the scroll of God's plan to see it through to completion. But now, in Yeshua the Messiah, we can surrender ourselves into His hands and obey Him, knowing that He will never abandon or betray us.

Lord, I surrender myself into your hands. Cover me and all my family with your infinite love and grace. Father, May Your Kingdom come and your will be done in my heart and throughout the earth.

Chapter 4 honours God the Father. He is the One who sits on the throne in heaven, and is the ultimate source of authority and praise. In Chapter 5 the attention suddenly shifts from God the Father to God the Son. The Bible teaches us that when we honour the Son we honour the Father. The Father has given all authority to His Son John 5:22. Scripture also teaches that the heavenly Father has given the Son a Kingdom, and it is His will that all creation, whether in heaven, on earth or under the earth, bow the knee to Christ as Lord of lords and King of kings Revelation 17:14, 19:16). This book is uniquely a revelation of Yeshua Messiah, demanding our absolute submission and praise. Therefore, from Chapter 5 to Chapter 22 we are constantly reminded of who is in charge. Jesus Christ alone has the ability to control the future.

Symbolism of the Lion of Judah

The very first lion Judah comes from the book of Genesis. Each of the Twelve Tribes of Israel has a symbol associated with it. For example, Benjamin is a wolf and Daniel is a snake. The verse in Genesis that gives the symbol of lion to Judah is: "Gur Aryeh Yehudah", which translates to "Young lion, Judah". Over time all Jews came to be known by the name Judah or Yehuda. It may at once be hard to understand why Judah would be so revered, considering his involvement in selling his brother Joseph into slavery. But as the story of Joseph comes to a conclusion, it becomes apparent why the Lion of Judah can be a symbol of the values and commitment of the Jewish people.

Judah and the Old Testament

The story of Joseph in the book of Genesis is full of lessons. Joseph is sold into slavery by his brothers but still somehow manages to rise to a powerful position in Egypt. After a devastating drought in the land of Canaan, Joseph's brothers come to beg him for food. They do not recognize him and do not suspect anything when he demands that they return back to him with their youngest brother Benjamin. Since the loss of Joseph, Benjamin has grown to become their father's favourite son and their father would rather not give him up. Judah promises his father that he will watch over Benjamin and will return safely home with him. Joseph ultimately is trying to teach his brothers a lesson and plants a silver cup in Benjamin's bag. The stolen cup is found and Joseph decrees that, as his punishment, Benjamin must stay in Egypt as his slave.

During this test of his brothers' character, Joseph is trying to see if his brothers will, once again, allow their brother to suffer so that they can improve their own lots in life. Judah comes forward, begging Joseph to allow his brother Benjamin to go free. He offers himself in his place.

Am I My Brother's Keeper?

Throughout Genesis, the question of a personal responsibility and responsibility for our neighbours is a central theme. From the story of Cain and Abel to the story of Joseph and his brothers' betrayal, this theme is underlying. Cain murders his brother Abel and casts off God's questions with a sarcastic response: "Am I My Brother's Keeper?" Cain shows no remorse or responsibility for what he has done. The rest of the book of Genesis represents the answer to that question and the answer is a resounding yes! Judah steps forward and takes responsibility. This results in the reuniting of his family. Yes, he is his brother's keeper and yes, he will take his place in slavery. With this passionate act, Judah becomes a role model for the responsibility that Jews have to each other and to the world as a whole.

The Lion of Judah and Tzedakah

The mitzvot of Tzedakah is closely intertwined with the Lion of Judah. Tzedakah represents the responsibility that each Jew has to be "their brother's keeper" and make a difference in the lives of others. Tzedakah literally translates to 'justice' and it involves making acts of devotion toward the needs of others a central focus in one's life. Whether it is a monetary gift or a gift of one's time, the power of the act of tzedakah cannot be overstated. The lion of Judah is a powerful symbol of this spirit of generosity and selflessness.

Who is Jesus? Is Jesus God? See what Jesus said about himself, his equality with God, and what exactly Jesus did to prove it.

It is impossible for us to know conclusively whether God exists and what he is like unless he takes the initiative and reveals himself.

We must scan the horizon of history to see if there is any clue to God's revelation. There is one clear clue. In an obscure village in Palestine, 2,000 years ago, a Child was born in a stable. Today the entire world is still celebrating the birth of Jesus, and for good reason.

Is Jesus God? Did Jesus ever claim to be God?

We're told that "the common people heard him gladly." And, "He taught as one who had authority, and not as their teachers of the Law."1 Is Jesus God? Did Jesus ever claim to be God? It soon became apparent, however, that he was making shocking and startling statements about himself. He began to identify himself as far more than a remarkable teacher or prophet. He began to say clearly that he was God. He made his identity the focal point of his teaching. The all important question he put to those who followed him was, "Who do you say I am?" When Peter answered and said, "You are the Christ, the Son of the living God,"2 Jesus was not shocked, nor did him rebuke Peter. On the contrary, he commended him! Jesus frequently referred to "My Father," and his hearers got the full impact of his words. We are told, "The Jews tried all the harder to kill him; not only was he breaking the Sabbath, but he was even calling God his own Father, making himself equal with God. On another occasion he said, "I and My Father are One." Immediately the religious authorities wanted to stone him. He asked them which of his good works caused them to want to kill him. They replied, "We are not stoning you for any of these but for blasphemy, because you, a mere man, claim to be God.

Is Jesus God? Look at His life.

As Jesus was healing a paralyzed man, Jesus said to him, "Son, your sins are forgiven you." The religious leaders immediately reacted. "Why does this fellow talk like that? He's blaspheming! Who can forgive sins but God alone? When Jesus was on trial for his life, the high priest put the question to him directly: "Are you the Christ, the Son of the Blessed One? "I am," said Jesus. "And you will see the Son of Man sitting at the right hand of the Mighty One and coming on the clouds of heaven."

The high priest rendered the verdict. "Why do we need any more witnesses?" he asked. "You have heard his blasphemy. So close was Jesus' connection with God that he equated a person's attitude to himself with the person's attitude toward God. Thus, to know him was to know God. To see him was to see God. To believe in him was to believe in God. To receive him was to receive God. To hate him was to hate God. And to honour him was to honour God.

Maybe Jesus lied when he said he was God. Perhaps he knew he was not God, but deliberately deceived his hearers. But there is a problem with this reasoning. Even those who deny his deity affirm that he was a great moral teacher. Jesus could hardly be a great moral teacher if, on the most crucial point of his teaching his identity he was a deliberate liar.

Another possibility is that Jesus was sincere but self-deceived. We have a name for a person today who thinks he is God. Mentally disabled. But as we look at the life of Christ, we see no evidence of the abnormality and imbalance we find in a mentally ill person. Rather, we find the greatest composure under pressure.

A third alternative is that his enthusiastic followers put words into his mouth he would have been shocked to hear. Were he to return, he would immediately repudiate them.

No, modern archaeology verifies that four biographies of Christ were written within the lifetime of people who saw, heard and followed Jesus. These gospel accounts contained specific facts and descriptions confirmed by those who were eyewitnesses of Jesus. The early writing of the Gospels by Matthew, Mark, Luke and John, is why they gained such circulation and impact, unlike the fictional Gnostic gospels which appeared centuries later.

Jesus was not a liar, or mentally disabled, or manufactured apart from historical reality. The only other alternative is that Jesus was being consciously truthful when he said he was God.

Is Jesus God? What is the proof?

From one point of view, however, claims don't mean much. Talk is cheap. Anyone can make claims. There have been others who have claimed to be God. I could claim to be God, and you could claim to be God, but the question all of us must answer is, "What credentials do we bring to substantiate our claim?" In my case it wouldn't take you five minutes to disprove my claim. It probably wouldn't take too much more to dispose of yours.

But when it comes to Jesus of Nazareth, it's not so simple. He had the credentials to back up his claim. He said, "Even though you do not believe me, believe the evidence of the miracles that you may learn and understand that the Father is in me, and I am in the Father.

The life of Jesus - His unique moral character

Is Jesus God? Did Jesus ever claim to be God? His moral character coincided with his claims. The quality of his life was such that he was able to challenge his very enemies with the question, "Can any of you prove me guilty of sin? He was met by silence, even though he addressed those who would have liked to point out a flaw in his character.

We read of Jesus being tempted by Satan, but we never hear of a confession of sin on his part. He never asked for forgiveness, though he told his followers to do so.

This lack of any sense of moral failure on Jesus' part is astonishing in view of the fact that it is completely contrary to the experience of the saints and mystics throughout the ages. The closer men and women draw to God, the more overwhelmed they are with their own failure, corruption, and shortcomings. The closer one is to a shining light, the more he realizes his need of a bath. This is true also, in the moral realm, for ordinary mortals.

It is also striking that John, Paul, and Peter, all of whom were trained from earliest childhood to believe in the universality of sin, all spoke of the sinlessness of Christ: "He committed no sin, and no deceit was found in his mouth. Even Pilate, who sentenced Jesus to death, asked, "What evil has he done?" After listening to the crowd, Pilate concluded, "I am innocent of this man's blood; see to it yourselves." The crowd relentlessly demanded Jesus crucified for blasphemy, claiming to be God. The Roman centurion who assisted in the crucifixion of Christ said, "Surely he was the Son of God.

The life of Jesus - He cured the sick

Jesus constantly demonstrated his power and compassion. He made the lame to walk, the blind to see, and healed those with diseases. For example, a man who had been blind from birth, Everyone knew him as the familiar beggar who sat outside the temple. Yet Jesus healed him. As the authorities questioned the beggar about Jesus, he said, "One thing I do know. I was blind but now I see!" he declared. He was astounded that these religious authorities didn't recognize this Healer as the Son of God. "Nobody has ever heard of opening the eyes of a man born blind," he said to him the evidence was obvious.

The life of Jesus - His ability to control nature

Jesus also demonstrated a supernatural power over nature itself. He commanded a raging storm of high wind and waves on the Sea of Galilee to be calm. Those in the boat were awestruck, asking, "Who is this? Even the wind and waves obey him! He turned water into wine, at a wedding. He fed a massive crowd of 5,000 people, starting with five loaves of bread and two fish. He gave a grieving widow back her only son by raising him from the dead.

Lazarus, a friend of Jesus' died and was buried in a tomb for four days already. Yet Jesus said, "Lazarus, come forth!" and dramatically raised him from the dead, witnessed by many. It is most significant that his enemies did not deny this miracle. Rather, they decided to kill him. "If we let him go on like this," they said, "everyone will believe in him.

Is Jesus God, as he claimed?

Is Jesus God? Did Jesus ever claim to be God? Jesus' supreme evidence of deity was his own resurrection from the dead. Five times in the course of his life, Jesus clearly predicted in what specific way he would be killed and affirmed those three days later he would rise from the dead.

Surely this was the great test. It was a claim that was easy to verify. It would either happen or not. It would either confirm his stated identity or destroy it. And significant for you and me, Jesus' rising from the dead would verify or make laughable statements such as these:

I am the way, the truth, and the life; no one comes to the Father except through me. I am the light of the world. He who follows me will not live in darkness, but will have the light of life. For those who believe in him, "I give them eternal life.

So by his own words, he offers this proof, The Son of Man is going to be delivered into the hands of men, and they will kill him. And when he is killed, after three days he will rise again.

What this would mean

Talk is cheap. Anyone can make claims. But when it comes to Jesus of Nazareth He had the credentials to back up His claim."

If Christ rose, we know with certainty that God exists, what God is like, and how we may know him in personal experience. The universe takes on meaning and purpose, and it is possible to experience the living God in this life.

On the other hand, if Christ did not rise from the dead, Christianity has no objective validity or reality. The martyrs who went singing to the lions, and contemporary missionaries who have given their lives while taking this message to others, have done extra ordinary job as his followers.

Paul, the great apostle, wrote, "If Christ has not been raised, our preaching is useless and so is your faith. Paul rested his whole case on the bodily resurrection of Christ. Did Jesus prove he is God? Let's look at the evidence for Jesus' resurrection.

Given all the miracles he had performed, Jesus easily could have avoided the cross, but he chose not to. Before his arrest, Jesus said, "I lay down my life that I may take it up again. No one takes it from me, but I lay it down of my own accord and I have authority to take it up again.

During his arrest, Jesus' friend Peter tried to defend him. But Jesus said to Peter, "Put your sword back into its place Do you think that I cannot appeal to my Father, and he will at once send me more than twelve legions of angels? He had that kind of power in heaven and on earth. Jesus went willingly to his death.

Jesus crucifixion and burial.

Jesus' death was by public execution on a cross, a common form of torture and death, used by the Roman government for many centuries. The accusation against Jesus was for blasphemy for claiming to be God. Jesus said it was to pay for our sin. Jesus was lashed with a multi-cord whip having metal or bone fragmented ends. A mock crown of long thorns was beaten into his skull. They forced him to walk to an execution hill outside of Jerusalem. They put him on a wooden cross, nailing his wrists and feet to it. He hung there, eventually dying. A sword was thrust into his side to confirm his death. The body of Jesus was taken from the cross, wrapped in mummy-like linens covered with gummy-wet spices. His body was placed in a solid rock tomb, where a very large boulder was rolled down to it, to secure the entrance. Everyone knew that Jesus said he would rise from the dead in three days. So they stationed a guard of trained Roman soldiers at the tomb. They also affixed an official Roman seal to the outside of the tomb declaring it government property.

Three days later, the tomb was empty. Is Jesus God? Did Jesus ever claim to be God? In spite of all this, three days later the boulder, formerly sealing the tomb, was found up a slope, some distance away from the tomb. The body was gone. Only the grave linens were found in the tomb, caved in, empty of the body.

It is important to note that both critics and followers of Jesus agree that the tomb was empty and the body missing. The earliest explanation circulated was that the disciples stole the body while the guards were sleeping. This makes little sense. This was an entire guard of highly trained Roman soldiers, and falling asleep on duty was punishable by death.

Further, each of the disciples individually and separately from each other were tortured and martyred for proclaiming that Jesus was alive, risen from the dead. Men and women will die for what they believe to be true, though it may actually be false. They do not, however, die for what they know is a lie. If ever a man tells the truth, it is on his deathbed.

Maybe the authorities moved the body? Yet they crucified Jesus to stop people from believing in him. This also is a weak possibility. If they had Christ's body, they could have paraded it through the streets of Jerusalem. In one fell swoop they would have successfully smothered Christianity in its cradle. That they did not do this bears eloquent testimony to the fact that they did not have the body.

Another theory is that the women, distraught and overcome by grief, missed their way in the dimness of the morning and went to the wrong tomb. In their distress they imagined Christ had risen because the tomb was empty. But again, if the women went to the wrong tomb, why did the high priests and other enemies of the faith not go to the right tomb and produce the body?

Men and women will die for what they believe to be true, though it may actually be false. They do not, however, die for what they know is a lie."

One other possibility is what some call "the swoon theory." In this view, Christ did not actually die. He was mistakenly reported to be dead, but had swooned from exhaustion, pain, and loss of blood, and in the coolness of the tomb, he revived. One would have to overlook the fact that they put a spear in his side to medically confirm his death.

But let us assume for a moment that Christ was buried alive and swooned. Is it possible to believe that he would have survived three days in a damp tomb without food or water or attention of any kind? Would he have had the strength to extricate himself from the grave clothes, push the heavy stone away from the mouth of the grave, overcome the Roman guards, and walk miles on feet that had been pierced with spikes? It too makes little sense. However, it wasn't the empty tomb that convinced Jesus' followers of his deity.

Not just the empty tomb.

That alone did not convince them that Jesus actually rose from the dead, was alive, and was God. What convinced them were the number of times that Jesus showed up, in person, in the flesh, and ate with them, and talked with them?

Luke, one of the gospel writers, says of Jesus, He presented himself to them and gave many convincing proofs that he was alive. He appeared to them over a period of forty days and spoke about the kingdom of God.

Is Jesus God?

All four of the gospel writers give accounts of Jesus physically showing up after his burial, obviously alive. One time that Jesus joined the disciples, Thomas, was not there. When they told him about it, Thomas simply wouldn't believe it. He flatly stated, "Unless I see the nail marks in his hands and put my finger where the nails were, and put my hand into his side, I will not believe it."

One week later, Jesus came to them again, with Thomas now present. Jesus said to Thomas, "Put your finger here; see my hands. Reach out your hand and put it into my side. Stop doubting and believe." Thomas replied, "My Lord and my God! Jesus told him "Because you have seen me, you have believed; blessed are those who have not seen and yet have believed.

Your opportunity why did Jesus go through all of that? It was so we could know God now, in this life, by believing in him. Jesus offers us a far more meaningful life, by being in a relationship with him. Jesus said, "I came that they might have life, and have it abundantly.

You can begin an intimate relationship with him right now. You can begin to personally know God in this life on earth, and after death into eternity. Here is God's promise to us: For God so loved the world, that he gave his only Son, that whoever believes in him should not perish but have eternal life.

Jesus took our sin on himself, on the cross. He chose to receive punishment for our sin, so that our sin would no longer be a barrier between us and him. Because he fully paid for your sin, he offers you complete forgiveness and a relationship with him.

Here is how you can begin that relationship. Jesus said, "Behold, I stand at the door of your heart and knock; if anyone hears my voice and opens the door, I will come into him. Right now you can invite Jesus Christ into your life. The words are not important. What matters is that you respond to him, in light of what he has done for you, and is now offering you. You could say to him something like, "Jesus, I believe in you. Thank you for dying on the cross for my sins. I ask you to forgive me and to come into my life right now. I want to know you and follow you. Thank you for coming into my life and giving me a relationship with you, right now. Thank you. If you asked Jesus come into your life, we would like to help you grow to know him better. In whatever way we can help you, please feel free to click on one of the links below at the end of this Book.

This is a really tricky question, isn't it! Many Christians have puzzled over this for many years, so it is pretty normal to struggle to understand how the relationship between God and Jesus works. I'm going to try to handle your questions in reverse order if that's ok. So the Bible tells us that Jesus isn't 'God's human son', rather, that Jesus, who is co-eternal with God that means that like God, he existed forever became human. Jesus was like God - eternal and perfect - but he became human so that he could enter into our world and die for humans. The Bible treats this as something to marvel at Jesus Christ 'though he was in the form of God, did not count equality with God a thing to be grasped, but made himself nothing, taking the form of a servant, being born in the likeness of men. And being found in human form, he humbled himself by becoming obedient to the point of death, even death on a cross. Philippians 2:6-8 The actual 'mechanics' of how God had a human son are not explained to us, but we are left in no doubt that Mary's conception and pregnancy are miraculous - you could read chapter 1 of the gospel of Luke to see the angel tell Mary that she will fall pregnant. The gospel of John, which was written in very symbolic language at the beginning, speaks about 'the word becoming flesh'. 'The word' is Jesus - who was with God in the beginning - and he became flesh this is what 'incarnate' means to be made flesh. This makes it clear that Jesus is the eternal God becoming human. So in answer to your second question, it isn't so much that God had a human son, but that God's son became human for our sake. So, to look at the first part of your question, what does it mean for God to have a son? Well, actually, when we say 'God' we could almost mean three people - God the Father, God the Son, or God the Holy Spirit. These three are called 'the trinity' and each one is called a 'person' of the trinity. It is quite hard to understand how these three works together. Some people find it easier to understand with an analogy so, for example, God is like water ice, water and steam are all water but they are all different. The analogy fails at various points but that might be a way to start to get your head around it. So a few things about the trinity that we should keep in mind; There is only one God so even as we talk about the three persons of the trinity we are talking about one God. All three persons of the trinity are God. If you want to look at some verses, you could look at Deuteronomy 6:4, Galatians 1:1, John 1:1-18, and Matthew 28:19.

There is relationship in the trinity the Son Jesus is obedient to the Father Luke 22:42; the Holy Spirit is sent by the Father and the Son John 16:15. So the three persons of the trinity are the same God but they are each distinct they have different roles, but each action any member of the trinity might do is God's action, regardless of who did it.

We see this distinction in unity when Jesus identifies himself with the Father, saying that he and the Father 'are one' John 10:38, 17:11, 21, and that he is in the Father and vice versa John 14:11. Jesus does not say that he IS the Father, or that he and the Father are the SAME, but that they are ONE. So they are distinct, yet unified. Because Jesus and the Father are both one and distinct, we can say that God 'sent his son into the world' - John 3:16, and also that Jesus came into the world 1 Tim 1:15 we are speaking about essentially the same action on the part of God, but on the one hand, God the Father sends, on the other, God the Son comes. We also see the distinction in unity at work when Jesus speaks about sending the Holy Spirit in John 16 - he describes this as both he and the Father coming. So the three persons of the trinity are distinct, but they are all God they all share the same motivations and objectives. They are all co-eternal, they are all perfect.

God is Father, Son, and Holy Spirit one God, existing in perfect relationship within him. This is how God can be both Father and Son because he just is! It's a bit unsatisfying to not wrap our heads around it more but if we want to have a right idea of who God is and what he is like, it's necessary to hold these strands together.

I hope this goes some way to answering everyone's question. A really helpful thing to do would be to read John 14-16, where Jesus explains some of this himself. In fact, why not John read from the beginning to get the picture of the whole gospel and how it builds together our picture of the relationship of the Son to the Father, especially as the Son came to earth as a man to reveal the Father to us. These are hard things to understand but well worth the mental effort! I wish you well in your efforts to understand these great things!

The Supremacy of the son of God Jesus quotes is Jesus God? Investigate these interesting claims others were convinced that Jesus was God:

Paul the apostle said Christ is the visible image of the invisible God.1John: and he existed in the beginning with God.2 Peter: "you must worship Christ as Lord of your life.

But what did Jesus say about himself? Did he ever identify himself as God? According to the Bible absolutely! Below are some of the statements he made. Jesus Said He Was Equal to God. Quotes from Jesus, Jesus Said He Existed before Abraham Your father Abraham rejoiced as he looked forward to my coming. He saw it and was glad.

The people said, "You aren't even fifty years old. How can you say you have seen Abraham? Jesus answered, "I tell you the truth, before Abraham was even I Am!"

Jesus Said to See Him is the same as Seeing God Jesus shouted to the crowds, if you trust me; you trust not only me, but also God who sent me. For when you see me, you are seeing the one who sent me. I have come as a light to shine in this dark world, so that all who put their trust in me will no longer remain in the dark.

No one can come to the Father except through me. If you had really known me, you would know who my Father is. From now on, you do know him and have seen him! Philip said, "Lord, show us the Father, and we will be satisfied."

Jesus replied, "Have I been with you all this time, Philip, and yet you still don't know who I am? Anyone who has seen me has seen the Father! So why are you asking me to show him to you? Jesus Said He Could Forgive Sins that you may know that the Son of Man has authority on earth to forgive sins" he then said to the paralytic Rise, pick up your bed and go home. And he rose and went home. When the crowds saw it, they were afraid, and they glorified God.

He said to them, You are from below; I am from above. You are of this world; I am not of this world. I told you that you would die in your sins, for unless you believe that I am he you will die in your sins.

Jesus Said He Is the Judge and Can Grant Eternal Life For as the Father raises the dead and gives them life, so also the Son gives life to which he will. The Father judges no one, but has given all judgment to the Son, that all may honour the Son, just as they honour the

Father. Jesus said to her, I am the resurrection and the life. Whoever believes in me, though he dies, yet shall he live My sheep hear my voice, and I know them, and they follow me. I give them eternal life, and they will never perish, and no one will snatch them out of my hand. For it is my Father's will that all who see his Son and believe in him should have eternal life. I will raise them up at the last day. Jesus Said He Was the Same as God the Father and I are one. Once again the people picked up stones to kill him.

Jesus said, at my Father's direction I have done many good works. For which one are you going to stone me? They replied, "We're stoning you not for any good work, but for blasphemy! You, a mere man, claim to be God. Jesus Said He Is Our Source for Life. Quotes from Jesus, I Am the Bread of Life

Jesus said to him, "I am the way, the truth, and the life. No one can come to the Father except through me. I am the light of the world. Whoever follows me will not walk in darkness, but will have the light of life If you abide in my word, you are truly my disciples, and you will know the truth, and the truth will set you free and Have life, abundantly. I am the good shepherd my sheep hear my voice, and I know them, and they follow me. I give them eternal life, and they will never perish, and no one will snatch them out of my hand.

He who loves me will be loved by my Father, and I will love him and manifest myself to him, If anyone loves me, he will keep my word, and my Father will love him, and we will come to him and make our home with him, always to the end of the age.

Here is little quotation to verify

Col 1:15, John 1:2, 1Peter 3:15, John 8:56-58, John 12:44-46, John 14:6-9, Matthew 9:6-8, John 8:23,24, John 5:21-23, John 11:25, John 10:27,28, John 6:40, John 10:30-33, John 6:35, John 14:6, John 8:12, John 8:31,32, John 10:10,27,28, John 14:21, Matthew 28:20

How can Jesus be both God and the Son of God?

Jesus can be both God and the son of God because the terms don't mean the same thing. When we say that Jesus is God John 1:1, 14; Colossians 2:9; Hebrews 1:8, we are saying that Jesus possesses the divine nature as well as a human nature, see hypostatic union. But the term "Son of God" does not mean that Jesus is not God. Think about it. If the term "Son of God" meant that Jesus is not God, then does the term "Son of Man" mean that Jesus is not a man?

Of course not. Likewise, if the term "Son of Man" means that Jesus is a man, then does it not imply that when it says Jesus is the "Son of God" that he is God? We ought not look at the ancient words found in Scripture and judge them by modern thinking. For this reason therefore the Jews were seeking all the more to kill Him, because He not only was breaking the Sabbath, but also was calling God His own Father, making Himself equal with God, John 5:18. As you can see in this verse, Jesus was calling God his own Father, making himself equal to God. Therefore, the term Son of God is a designation of the equality with God when it is a reference to Christ. Jesus is the Son of God The phrase "Son of God" occurs 44 times in the New American Standard Bible. Each time it is used of Christ. It is a title of his pre-eminence, holiness, and relationship to God the Father. In fact, we see that the Pharisees wanted to kill him for proclaiming he was the son of God I and the Father are one. The Jews picked up stones again to stone Him. Jesus answered them, "I showed you many good works from the Father; for which of them are you stoning me? The Jews answered Him, For a good work we do not stone you, but for blasphemy; and because you, being a man, make yourself out to be God. Jesus answered them, Has it not been written in your Law, 'I SAID, YOU ARE GODS'? If he called them gods, to whom the word of God came and the Scripture cannot be broken, do you say of Him, whom the Father sanctified and sent into the world, 'You are blaspheming,' because I said, 'I am the Son of God'?" John 10:30-36.

In this account we see the second instance of Jesus being threatened with stoning. The first one is a little earlier.

"Jesus said to them, 'Truly, truly, I say to you, before Abraham was born, I am.' 59 Therefore they picked up stones to throw at Him, but Jesus hid Himself and went out of the temple, John 8:58-59.

Jesus' words here are significant because he says he is the "I am." This is similar to what is found in Exodus.

God said to Moses, "I AM WHO I AM"; and He said, Thus you shall say to the sons of Israel, 'I AM has sent me to you. God, furthermore, said to Moses, Thus you shall say to the sons of Israel, 'The LORD, the God of your fathers, the God of Abraham, the God of Isaac, and the God of Jacob, has sent me to you.' This is my name forever, and this is my memorial-name to all generations, Exodus 3:14-15.

When we combine all of this together we see that Jesus was claiming the divine title for himself John 8:58; Exodus 3:14-15 and that is why the Jews wanted to kill him (John 8:59 and John 10:31). The explanation given is that Jesus was claiming equality with God by claiming that he was the Son of God.

So, when we say that Jesus is God we are saying that he is divine by nature. He is, after all, the second person of the Trinity. But when we say that Jesus is the Son of God, we are saying that he is also God since that is what the phrase means.

Bible verses related to Acknowledging God from the King James Version (KJV) by Relevance - Sort By Book Order

Proverbs 3:5-6 - Trust in the LORD with all thine heart; and lean not unto thine own understanding.

Revelation 4:11 - Thou art worthy, O Lord, to receive glory and honour and power: for thou hast created all things, and for thy pleasure they are and were created.

Acts 10:1-48 - There was a certain man in Caesarea called Cornelius, a centurion of the band called the Italian band,

Psalms 115:16 - The heaven, even the heavens, are the LORD'S: but the earth hath he given to the children of men.

Genesis 1:3-31 - And God said, Let there be light: and there was light. Joshua 1:3 - Every place that the sole of your foot shall tread upon, that have I given unto you, as I said unto Moses.

Romans 1:28-31 - And even as they did not like to retain God in their knowledge, God gave them over to a reprobate mind, to do those things which are not convenient.

Christ The Deliverer

Shall the prey be taken from the mighty, or the lawful captive delivered? The Lord: Even the captives of the mighty shall be taken away, and the prey of the terrible shall be delivered: for I will contend with him that coutendeth with thee, and I will save thy children. Isaiah 49: 24, 26.

You find in these verses what Christ came to do. He did not come to preach elegant sermons: He came to the world to proclaim liberty to the captive. Every soul in this building is either under the power of the prince of this world and doing his bidding, or he is brought out of this old kingdom and is brought into the kingdom of the Lord Jesus Christ.

There are only two classes in this world. You must be either for the Lord or against him. There may be some persons here who are not Christians, who are saying to them, I am not under the power of Satan. I will do as I please. Satan has no power over me; I do as it pleases me. If there is an unconverted person here who has that idea, I can tell him it is a false one. You cannot hold a more false impression than that. I can prove to you that it is false. Have you not some sins that trouble you? And you try and break off that sin?" and have you not tried and tried, and failed every time? And could not you, if you were honest tonight, write "failure" over every attempt you nave made to reform yourself? Satan binds every one of us. If we have not been liberated by Christ, we are still under his power. Every one of us has some besetting sin; and Satan knows our weak point and can holds us: and we have no power to liberate ourselves. We cannot give ourselves liberty. A great many do not want to become Christians, because they do not want to give up their liberty, but the greatest slaves in the world are the slaves of the devil. They are under his power; they cannot do as they please; they have not the power to do as they please. When we had slavery in our country, if a slave had a wife she also is a slave, all their children are born into slavery. Every one of us is born into slavery to Satan, by nature. In sin did my mother conceive me. We cannot talk about liberty until we know Christ. We see the old nature in children, even when one year old. We see the child's will rises against their parents or mother's will; that is their under the very power of the evil one. How many young men in this assembly have tried to break off some of their habits that are taking them down to ruin, and sinking them lower and lower? They have tried to get the victory over them; but they have failed. How many have been in the inquiry-room daring these past weeks, and told us how they have tried to break off old habits and failed every time? They have said: "It is an awful hard thing to be a Christian. I have tried to serve God and failed." It is utterly impossible for you to serve God until you get liberty in Christ until you get power over Satan. I do not know what your besetting sin is; but every man and woman in this assembly, out of Christ, has some besetting sin, and Satan holds you with that sin. He holds some by the power of strong drink; others by their tempers; and others by profanity. Satan does not care which way he takes you to hell, if he only gets you there at last. He has all men in his power who have not been liberated by Jesus Christ. Christ says, He came to proclaim liberty. That is his proclamation; and there is not a slave of the devil to-night but what may be set free. No one but Christ has the power to set the sinner free. That is why the Gospel is good news: it is good news because it proclaims liberty to the captive.

In the days of Wilberforce, there was an effort made to get a bill through the British parliament to give liberty to the slaves held by their masters in those West India islands belonging to Great Britain.

Those poor fugitives were anxious to hear the decision of parliament upon that question. They could not telegraph over the water, as we can now; but they were watching for a vessel to come in. At last a vessel came in to one of those islands. The captain could not wait until he got on shore to proclaim the news of freedom; but he shouted at the top of bids voice, as loud as he could cry: "Free! free! fret!" The people took up the cry, and it rung all through the island: "'Free I free I free" They were no longer slaves that was the proclamation. Jesus Christ comes from the throne of God, and he proclaims liberty to every slave of the devil. If there is one here in this assembly whom the devil holds in slavery, he can be free if he will only come to Christ.

When I was returning from Europe in 1872, 1 met Governor Curtin on board the steamer coming back from Russia. I was much interested in the account he gave of the Emperor having liberated forty million serfs. We thought President Lincoln had done a great "ring when he liberated our slaves; but it was far surpassed by the action of the Emperor of Russia. He called his imperial council together, to endeavour to devise some way by which liberty could be given to these serfs. They assembled, and consulted together for six long months; and at last, one night, they sent in word to the Emperor that it would not be expedient to liberate them that it was not best to liberate them. That night the Emperor went to the Greek church and partook of the sacrament. The next morning he ordered his guards up with their guns; they guarded the palace, and planted tear cannon for a protection. At midday a ukase was sent forth by the Emperor, proclaiming liberty to forty million serfs. They were made 'free. That is the proclamation I bring you tonight, and what you want to-night is just to believe the proclamation. It is not bad news; it is good news.

During our war, a number of our men were taken prisoners by the Southern army. These prisoners were very anxious to be released; they waited anxiously to hear the news that prisoners were to be exchanged. At one prison nine hundred men were confined. Word was brought to them one day that every man with the rank of captain was to be taken to the commanding officer's office. The prisoners thought that these captains were to be sent home. Then every colonel wished he was a captain. He would like to come down in the ranks; and every lieutenant wished he was higher up. They were all congratulating these captains, for they thought they were going back to their wives and mothers, and they had been suffering in that prison for a long time. They were taken to the commanding officer's office; they were all silent; all of them expected to be paroled out. The commanding officer said: "I have painful news to tell. I am ordered to select two of you for immediate execution." The feeling that came over that company was something awful. The officers proceeded to put the names of these captains into a hat; one of them then put his hand into the hat, and brought out the names of two men. He read the names he had drawn they were Sawyer and Flynn. The hair of one of these men turned grey during the next night. Our government heard what was going on, and they sent this word to Richmond: "You take the lives of those men, and we will take the life of the nephew of General Lee." All at once news came to these two captains, "You are going to be saved." Do you think that was not good news to them? Now, you know you are under the sentence of death. We are all condemned to die? the sentence is already out against us. And now comes liberty for every poor captive that wants it. If you want liberty, this is how you can have it.

I will give you another illustration. We will look into Libby prison and see those one thousand men there, some of them dying for want of care. The news comes to them: "General Lee has been defeated, and has been driven in from his outer works." What news it must have been to those poor men. By and by they receive other news; they hear that Richmond has been taken. How jubilant they are? By and by they can hear our Union soldiers coming down the streets of Richmond; they can hear the band playing the tune of "The Star Spangled Banner." Soon they throw open the prison doors, and the captives are free. I came to-night to proclaim liberty to the captive. If Satan has you bound to-night by some terrible in, the Son of God will set you free. He has the keys of heaven and hell. He will deliver you this night, if you will let him in.

A parable was told by Mr Spurgeon of a tyrant. who ordered one of his subjects, a blacksmith, into his presence, and said to him: "Make a chain of a certain length, and bring it to me on a certain day." The blacksmith returned on a certain day, with the chain of certain length. The tyrant said: "Make it twice as long and bring it to me." The blacksmith made it, and brought it to him. The tyrant said again: "Make it twice the length, and bring it to me." The third time the man made the chain twice its former length, and brought it back. The tyrant then said to his officers: Take that chain, and bind that man hand and foot. That is what the devil is going to do with you. He is making you forget your own chain. What you want to night is to become free. I do not care how dark the sin may be, you can be free.

There is no class of sinners in Philadelphia but is represented in this Bible. One man says: I am a thief; and if I am converted, I will have to make restitution. It is the best thing you can do. Some may say: I have not the power to make restitution; I have squandered the money. Then go and confess it, and the man whom you have wronged will have compassion on you. You may say, I am afraid he will put me in prison. I never knew a man but had mercy on the man that confessed to him that he had wronged him, and asked his forgiveness. A minister told me of a man whose conscience was aroused under the sermon, and he said to the minister: I am a clerk in such a store, and I have stolen five hundred dollars. I want to become a Christian; but that is standing in my way, and tarring me in the face. I have had no peace of mind for a long time. I have not got the money, and I cannot make restitution. Says the minister: Why don't you go to your employer and tell him? The young man said, He will put me in prison. The minister «aid: I would make a clean breast of it. Go to him and tell him all about it. It is better for you to do right than to do wrong. You have done wrong; don't conceal it and you will get liberty. The minister could not get the young man to consent to go. At last he said: I will go and talk with your employer, if you will allow me. The young man gave him permission. He went to the counting room of the young man's employer, and told him all about it, and laid: I have faith to believe that man is reformed, and if you will forgive him you will find him a good clerk. The merchant said, I will not speak to him about it. He did not discharge him; he kept him in his old place, and he turned out to be the best man in the place. Many a man thinks he cannot get freedom because he is bound in that way. The Lord Jesus Christ will give you victory. If you will confess your sin, he will give you victory. That is what he came to do: to proclaim liberty to the captive. As long as a man living in sin, there is no liberty; but the moment you come to Jesus Christ and confess to him, he will sweep your sins out of the way, and the clear light of Calvary will burst across your path.

How many men are so guilty that they cannot look in your eye; and yet these men talk about liberty, and do not want to become Christians because they do not want to give up liberty. You never will know what true liberty is until you come to Christ. If you confess your sins, Christ will give you pure liberty; and peace and joy will flow over your soul like a river. Look over the list of those who have been saved, as recorded in the Bible; and see how many have been saved when they came to the Lord and confessed their sins. When you confess your sins, the Lord is ready to forgive you. If there is a sin sick soul here to-night, if you will be honest and go and confess your sin, he will take it away, and bring your soul out of that dark prison it is in. I would much rather have my body in prison than my soul. It is better to have the soul safe with God and save the body in prison, than to have the soul in prison and the body under the power of the devil. Look at poor Barabbas in prison in Jerusalem. He is counting the hours when he will be led out to execution. He has had his trial and been found guilty. The laws have condemned him to die the death of the cross; the day is set for his execution; the hour will soon come. I can imagine the night before the day appointed for his execution he did not sleep; I can imagine he did not eat anything; I see him trembling from head to foot, because he is going to meet God. Bear in mind that the time may be very short to some of us. A man who was here last night said to a friend, I am coming to-morrow into the inquiry-room. He fell dead twenty minutes before three o'clock this afternoon. Christ has proclaimed liberty to every captive. Poor Barabbas; he knows his hour is coming; perhaps he is counting the minutes. He says, So many minutes, and I will be gone. They had a man executed a few years ago in Chicago, and they put up the scaffold in the jail. It troubled him very much to hear them putting up the scaffold, because it brought the thought to him that he was to be led out and executed. Poor Barabbas might have heard the carpenters working on the cross, and he might have said, In a few hours I am to be led out. The great iron door of the prison swung open and the executioner says to him, Barabbas, you are free. Barabbas says what! Free I Yes, you are going to your wife and children. What does it mean? I free! My God! What does it mean? I have not to die no more? The executioner says, the people have chosen Jesus of Nazareth to die in your place. That is substitution. Barabbas was the man that ought to die; his hand was trickling with the blood of his fellow men. Jesus came to set the captive free. Every man that has committed sin is a lawful captive. The soul that sinneth, it shall die. Here is Christ dying in the place of Barabbas; he has gone up on high; he loves and intercedes for you; he has power to proclaim liberty to every poor bondman upon the earth. He went to the temple, one day, and there was a poor woman there who had been bound by Satan for eighteen years.

PHILIP ODEI TETTEY

Christ Our Saviour

Jesus Christ is the Saviour of the world and the Son of God. He is our Redeemer. Each of these titles points to the truth that Jesus Christ is the only way by which we can return to live with our Heavenly Father.

Jesus suffered and was crucified for the sins of the world, giving each of God's children the gift of repentance and forgiveness. Only by His mercy and grace can anyone be saved. His subsequent Resurrection prepared the way for every person to overcome physical death as well. These events are called the Atonement. In short, Jesus Christ saves us from sin and death. For that, He is very literally our Saviour and Redeemer.

In the future Jesus Christ will return to reign on earth in peace for a thousand years. Jesus Christ is the Son of God, and He will be our Lord forever. Members of The Church of Jesus Christ of Latter-day Saints have always worshipped God the Eternal Father in the name of Jesus Christ. When asked what the Latter-day Saints believe, Joseph Smith put Christ at the centre: The fundamental principles of our religion is the testimony of the apostles and prophets concerning Jesus Christ, 'that he died, was buried, and rose again the third day, and ascended up into heaven;' and all other things [pertaining to our religion] are only appendages to these." The modern-day Quorum of the Twelve Apostles reaffirmed that testimony when they proclaimed: "Jesus is the Living Christ, the immortal Son of God. ... His way is the path that leads to happiness in this life and eternal life in the world to come."

Christ Our Redeemer

I testify that the Lord came into the world that he may save all men if they will hearken unto his voice that He suffered the pains of all men, and that He was crucified that the resurrection might pass upon all men, that all might stand before him at the great and judgment day. I witness that he commanded all men that they must repent, and be baptized in his name, having perfect faith in Him or they cannot be saved in the kingdom of God. Repent, be baptized, and have perfect faith in Him. These are some of the essential requirements that must be met. I know that there is no other way nor means whereby man can be saved, only through the atoning blood of Jesus Christ. I witness that Jesus Christ atoned for the sins of the world, to bring about the plan of mercy, to appease the demands of justice that God might be a perfect, just God, and a merciful God also. I testify that except for the Atonement of the Holy Redeemer, the demands of justice would prevent every soul born on earth from returning to the presence

Of God, to be partakes of His glory and exaltation, for all make mistakes for which we cannot personally appease justice. I witness that except for the infinite atonement" of Christ, we could not return to God after death and, as Jacob solemnly warned, our spirits would become subject to the devil, so we rise no more. And our spirits would become like unto him, and we would become devils, angels to a devil, to be shut out from the presence of our God, to remain with the father of lies, in misery.

I witness that redemption cometh in and through the Holy Messiah; unto all those who have a broken heart and a contrite spirit; and unto none else can the ends of the law be answered. This is absolute requisite of a broken heart and a contrite spirit prescribes the need to be submissive, compliant, humble that is, teachable, and willingly obedient. Finally, I witness how great the importance to make these things known unto the inhabitants of the earth, that they may know that there is no flesh that can dwell in the presence of God, save it be through the merits, and mercy, and grace of the Holy Messiah.

Jesus Christ possessed merits that no other child of Heavenly Father could possibly have. He was a God, Jehovah, before His birth in Bethlehem. His Father not only gave Him His spirit body, but Jesus was His Only Begotten Son in the flesh. Our Master lived a perfect, sinless life and therefore was free from the demands of justice. He was and is perfect in every attribute, including love, compassion, patience, obedience, forgiveness, and humility. His mercy pays our debt to justice when we repent and obey Him. Even with our best efforts to obey His teachings we will still fall short, yet because of His grace we will be saved "after all we can do.

Although our memory of it is withheld, before we came to this earth we lived in the presence of God, our Eternal Father, and His Son, Jesus Christ. We shouted for joy when given the privilege of coming to this earth to receive a body and to move forward in God's plan for our happiness. We knew that we would be tested here. Our determination was to live obediently to be able to return to be with our Father forever. Part of that testing here is to have so many seemingly interesting things to do that we can forget the main purposes for being here. Satan works very hard so that the essential things won't happen.

The plan is really very simple when considered in its essence. The Lord has told us that we are here to be tried to be proven, to see whether we will be valiant and be obedient to His teachings. You among all of the people on earth have the best possibility of doing that because you have access to the fullness of the restored gospel and the teachings of the Saviour. In quiet moments when you think about it, you recognize what is critically important in life and what isn't. Be wise and don't let good things crowd out those that are essential. What are the essential ones? They are related to doctrine. They are cantered in ordinances and embrace critical covenants. Those ordinances are baptism and confirmation into His Church and kingdom on earth. For men they include worthy ordination to the Melchizedek Priesthood and honouring and using it in service to others. For each adult man and woman, they entail all of the ordinances of the temple, including one's own personal endowment. They embody the sealing ordinance of the temple where a man and wife are bound so that through obedience they can live together for time and all eternity. When faithful, the children born to that union or later sealed to their parents are joined in love and rejoicing throughout all eternity. To receive all of the blessings of His atoning sacrifice, we are only asked to be obedient to His commandments and to receive all of these essential ordinances. The Atonement will not only help us overcome our transgressions and mistakes, but in His time, it will resolve all inequities of life those things that are unfair which are the consequences of circumstance or others' acts and not our own decisions.

While some may not understand or agree, I testify that it is not sufficient to be baptized and then live an acceptable life, avoiding major transgressions. The Lord has decreed that the additional ordinances and covenants that I have mentioned must be received for exaltation and eternal life. Being worthy of temple ordinances means that you will choose to do what many in the world are not willing to do. You will keep the Sabbath day holy, exercise faith through the payment of tithing and fast offerings, consistently participate in Church worship, give service, and show love and appreciation for your family by helping each member of it. After you have received all of the temple ordinances, you will continue to grow by keeping the covenants made and faithfully "enduring to the end.

Keeping the covenants is not hard when you do it willingly with a broken heart and a contrite spirit, when obeyed; those covenants bring happiness and joy. They give purpose to life. Difficulty comes when agency is used to make choices that are inconsistent with those covenants. Study the things you do in your discretionary time, that time you are free to control. Do you find that it is cantered in those things that are of highest priority and of greatest importance? Or do you unconsciously, consistently fill it with trivia and activities that are not of enduring value nor help you accomplish the purpose for which you came to earth? Think of the long view of life, not just what's going to happen today or tomorrow. Don't give up what you most want in life for something you think you want now. The essential things must be accomplished during your testing period on earth. They must have first priority. They must not be sacrificed for lesser things, even though they are good and worthwhile accomplishments. After this life, you will be restored to that which you have here allowed yourself to become. Oh, if I but had the capacity to communicate the peace and serenity that come from knowing that you and your family have worthily received all of the saving ordinances and the corresponding covenants are being righteously kept. I encourage you with every capacity that I possess to receive all of the ordinances for salvation and do all you can to have the other members of your family receive those ordinances before departing this earth. You can progress much more rapidly here on earth with your mortal body in this environment of good and evil than you will as a spirit in the spirit world. Compared to the length of a normal life, it doesn't take much time to receive all of the ordinances essential to exaltation. It does take diligence, understanding, and obedience. It does require you to do all within your capacity to qualify for those ordinances and to receive as many as you are able. Where, for reasons beyond your control, you are not able to receive them all, live worthily and do not disqualify yourself through neglect, indifference, or unworthiness. The Lord will make it possible for you to receive all of the blessings He has promised in His time and place.

Whether you intend to or not, when you live as though the Saviour and His teachings are only one of many other important priorities in your life, you are clearly on the road to disappointment and likely on the path to tragedy. Is it really wise to forfeit eternal happiness by fulfilling only part of the requirements? I pray that you'll be moved to make needed changes now.

If you have strayed in transgression, please come back. If you have been enticed by the things of the world to forget the things of God, correct your priorities. If you haven't received all of the essential ordinances, decide now to do what is necessary to receive them. OH, how grateful we must be for the Atonement wrought by our Redeemer, Jesus Christ! It gives life richness and joy when we live the pattern described in this scripture:

They did fast and pray often, and did wax stronger and stronger in their humility, and firmer and firmer in the faith in Christ, unto the filling their souls with joy and consolation, yea, even to the purifying and the sanctification of their hearts, which sanctification cometh because of their yielding their hearts unto God.

I witness that remission of sins through the Atonement bringeth meekness, and lowliness of heart; and because of meekness and lowliness of heart cometh the visitation of the Holy Ghost, which Comforter filleth with hope and perfect love. I testify that God, your Eternal Father, loves you. He hears your prayers and will answer them. The Redeemer loves you and will help you do the essential things that bring happiness now and forever. I am a witness of Jesus Christ. I know that He lives. By calling Christ our Redeemer, we confess the fact that we are, by nature, sold into a three-fold bondage to sin, to the corruption of this cursed world, and to the devil. We are born into the long, slow advance of a slave's death and the multiplied miseries that accompany it. By nature, death is our master and destiny.

Second, by calling Christ our Redeemer, we confess that we cannot free ourselves from our bondage to sin, misery and death. We lack the capacity and the will. We confess that we are indeed sick, sick unto death, in need of a divine physician. Third, by calling Christ our Redeemer, we confess that Jesus of Nazareth alone was able to pay the great price, the ransom, for our freedom. That price was the suffering of an innocent substitute himself freely offered to satisfy the justice of God's wrath against sin. By offering himself in our place, the just for the unjust, Christ has set us free from the penalty and power of sin, the world, and the devil. As a result, life, not death, is our eternal destiny.

Do you sense in your soul the enslaving power of sin and death working in you? Rejoice! For Christ, your Redeemer has bought your life for God, and He rejoices to receive you.

For even the Son of Man came not to be served but to serve, and to give his life as a ransom for many Mark 10:45 I hope this reminder will fan the flames of prayer and worship in your heart. May you grasp how high and deep and wide is the love of God for you in giving His only Son, your Redeemer, to rescue you from your hopeless estate so that you might belong to God.

Why do we call Christ our Mediator?

By calling Christ our mediator, we confess first the fact of our natural alienation from God, our state of enmity with him, and our inability to approach His Majesty on our own merits. Our inability is due not only to our moral bondage to sin, but also to God's curse upon sin. Like Adam, we have been driven out of His presence, cursed, banished. Therefore, we cannot return to God's favour unless one whom God favours intercedes for us and reconciles us to Him.

Second, by calling Christ our Mediator, we confess that God has mercifully appointed a mediator for us of His own choosing. He has not left us without hope in the world; He has not utterly locked the door upon us. However, a mediated relationship with God is the only possibility of an amiable relationship with Him. No one comes to the Father except through me.–John 14:6b

Third, by calling Christ our Mediator, we confess that Jesus of Nazareth is the only mediator between us and God. He is God's chosen man. He alone represents us before God, and we have no say in the terms of our return. We bring nothing to a bargaining table. No, we are brought to a banquet table of God's favour, by Christ, and for his sake. He alone can heal the breach and reconcile us to God; and in rejecting him, we remain under God's curse.

Do you sense in your soul the infinite divide between you and God? Rejoice! For Christ, your Mediator has brought you in peace to God, and He rejoices to receive you. For there is one God, and one mediator between God and men, the man Christ Jesus.–1 Timothy 2:5

Their Call and Ordination

The night preceding the morn on which the Twelve Apostles were called and ordained was spent by the Lord in solitary seclusion; He had "continued all night in prayer to God Then, when day had come, and while many people were gathering to hear more of the new and wonderful gospel of the kingdom, He called to come closer some who had theretofore been devotedly associated together as His disciples or followers, and from among them He chose twelve, whom he ordained and named apostles' Prior to that time none of these had been distinguished by any special delegation of authority or appointment; they had been numbered with the disciples in general, though, as we have seen, seven had received a preliminary call, and had promptly responded thereto by abandoning wholly or in part their business affairs, and had followed the Master. These were Andrew, John, Simon Peter, Philip, Nathanael, James, and Levi Matthew. Prior to this eventful day, however, none of the Twelve had been ordained or set apart to their sacred office.

The three Gospel writers who make record of the organization of the twelve tribes, Simon Peter first and Judas Iscariot last in the category; they agree also in the relative position of some but not of all the others. Following the order given by Mark, and this may be the most convenient since he was named as the first three those who later became most prominent, we have the following list: Simon Peter, James son of Zebedee, John brother of the last-named, Andrew brother of Simon Peter, Philip, Bartholomew or Nathanael, Matthew, Thomas, James son of Alpheus, Judas also known as Lebbeus or Thaddeus, Simon distinguished by his surname Zelotes, also known as the Canaanite, and Judas Iscariot.

The Twelve Considered Individually

Simon, named as the first apostle, is more commonly known as Peter the appellation given him by the Lord on the occasion of their first meeting, and afterward confirmed He was the son of Joan, or Jonas, and by vocation was a fisherman. He and his brother Andrew were partners with James and John, the sons of Zebedee; and apparently the fishing business was a prosperous one with them, for they owned their boats and gave employment to other men's Peter's early home had been at the little fishery town of Bethsaida on the west shore of the Sea of Galilee; but about the time of his first association with Jesus, or soon thereafter, he, with others of his family, removed to Capernaum, where he appears to have become an independent householder's Simon Peter was a married man before his call to the ministry. He was well to do in a material way; and when he once spoke of having left all to follow Jesus, the Lord did not deny that Peter's sacrifice of temporal possessions was as great as had been implied. We are not justified in regarding him as unlettered or ignorant. True, both he and John were designated by the council of rulers as unlearned and ignorant men, but this was spoken of them as indicating their lack of training in the schools of the rabbis; and it is worthy to note, that the members of that same council were amazed at the wisdom and power manifested by the two apostles, whom they professed to despise.

In temperament Peter was impulsive and stern, and, until trained by severe experience, was lacking in firmness. He had many human weaknesses, yet in spite of them all he eventually overcame the temptations of Satan and the frailties of the flesh, and served his Lord as the appointed and acknowledged leader of the Twelve. Of the time and place of his death the scriptures do not speak; but the manner thereof was prefigured by the resurrected Lord, and in part was foreseen by Peter himself. Tradition, originating in the writings of the early Christian historians other than the apostles, states that Peter met death by crucifixion as a martyr during the persecution incident to the reign of Nero, probably between A.D. 64 and 68. Origen states that the apostle was crucified with his head downward. Peter, with James and John, his associates in the presidency of the Twelve, has ministered as a resurrected being in the present dispensation, in restoring to earth the Melchizedek Priesthood, including the Holy Apostleship, which had been taken away because of the apostasy and unbelief of men.

James and John, brothers by birth, partners in business as fishermen, brethren in the ministry, were associated together and with Peter in the apostolic calling. The Lord bestowed upon the pair a title in common Boanerges, or Sons of Thunder possibly with reference to the zeal they developed in His service, which, indeed, at times had to be restrained, as when they would have had fire called from heaven to destroy the Samaritan villagers who had refused hospitality to the Master. They and their mother aspired to the highest honours of the kingdom, and asked that the two be given places, one on the right the other on the left of Christ in His glory. This ambition was gently reproved by the Lord, and the request gave offense to the other apostles. With Peter these two brothers were witnesses of many of the most important incidents in the life of Jesus; thus, the three were the only apostles admitted to witness the raising of the daughter of Jairus from death to life; they were the only members of the Twelve present at the transfiguration of Christly they were nearest the Lord during the period of His mortal agony in Gethsemane and, as heretofore told, they have ministered in these modern days in the restoration of the Holy Apostleship with all its ancient authority and power of blessing. James is commonly designated in theological literature as James I, to distinguish him from the other apostle bearing the same name. James, the son of Zebedee, was the first of the apostles to meet a martyr's violent death; he was beheaded by order of the king, Herod Agrippa. John had been a disciple of the Baptist, and had demonstrated his confidence in the latter's testimony of Jesus by promptly turning from the forerunner and following the Lord. He became a devoted servant, and repeatedly refers to himself as the disciple "whom Jesus loved. At the last supper John sat next to Jesus leaning his head upon the Master's breast; and next day as he stood beneath the cross he received from the dying Christ the special charge to care for the Lord's mother; and to this he promptly responded by conducting the weeping Mary to his own house. He was the first to recognize the risen Lord on the shores of Galilee, and received from His immortal lips encouragement of his hope that his life would be continued in the body, in order that he might minister among men until the Christ shall come in His glory. The realization of that hope has been attested by revelation in modern day Christians.

Andrew, son of Jona and brother of Simon Peter, is mentioned less frequently than the three already considered. He had been one of the Baptist's followers, and with John, the son of Zebedee, left the Baptist to learn from Jesus; and having learned he went in search of Peter, solemnly averred to him that the Messiah had been found, and brought his brother to the Saviour's feet. He shared with Peter in the honour of the call of the Lord on the sea shore, and in the promise "I will make you fishers of men." In one instance we read of Andrew as present with Peter, James and John, in a private interview with the Lord; and he is mentioned in connection with the miraculous feeding of the five thousand, and as associated with Philip in arranging an interview between certain inquiring Greeks and Jesus. He is named with others in connection with our Lord's ascension. Tradition is rife with stories about this man, but of the extent of his ministry, the duration of his life, and the circumstances of his death, we have authentic record.

Philip may have been the first to receive the authoritative call "Follow me" from the lips of Jesus, and we find him immediately testifying that Jesus was the long expected Messiah. His home was in Bethsaida, the town of Peter, Andrew, James, and John. It is said that Jesus found him, whereas the others concerned in that early affiliation seem to have come of themselves severally to Christ. We find brief mention of him at the time the five thousand were fed, on which occasion Jesus asked him "Whence shall we buy bread, that these may eat?" This was done to test and prove him, for Jesus knew what would be done. Philip's reply was based on a statement of the small amount of money at hand, and showed no expectation of miraculous intervention. It was to him the Greeks applied when they sought a meeting with Jesus as noted in connection with Andrew. He was mildly reproved for his misunderstanding when he asked Jesus to show to him and the others the Father, Jesus replied "Have I been so long time with you, and yet hast thou not known me, Philip? Aside from incidental mention of his presence as one of the Eleven after the ascension, the scriptures tell us nothing more concerning him.

Bartholomew is mentioned in scripture by this name only in connection with his ordination to the apostleship, and as one of the Eleven after the ascension. The name means son of Tolmai. It is practically certain, however, that he is the man called Nathanael in John's Gospel the one whom Christ designated as "an Israelite indeed, in whom is no guile." He is named again as among those who went fishing with Peter after the resurrection of Christ. His home was in Cana of Galilee. The reasons for assuming that Bartholomew and Nathanael are the same person are these: Bartholomew is named in each of the three synoptic Gospels as an apostle, but Nathanael is not mentioned. Nathanael is named twice in John's Gospel, and Bartholomew not at all; Bartholomew and Philip, or Nathanael and Philip, are mentioned together.

Matthew, or Levi, son of Alpheus was one of the seven who received a call to follow Christ before the ordination of the Twelve. He was the one who gave a feast, for attending which Jesus and the disciples were severely criticized by the Pharisees, on the charge that it was unseemly for Him to eat with publicans and sinners. Matthew was a publican; he so designates himself in the Gospel he wrote; but the other evangelists omitted him and did not mention when including him with the Twelve. His Hebrew name, Levi, is understood by many as an indication of priestly lineage. Of his ministry we have no detailed account though he is the author of the first Gospel; he refrains from special mention of himself except in connection with his call and ordination. He is spoken of by other than scriptural writers as one of the most active of the apostles after Christ's death and as operating in lands far from Palestine.

Thomas, also known as Didymus, the Greek equivalent of his Hebrew name, meaning a twin, is mentioned as a witness of the raising of Lazarus. His devotion to Jesus was shown by his desire to accompany the Lord to Bethany, though persecution in that region was almost certain. To his fellow apostles Thomas said: Let us also go that we may die with him. Even as late in his experience as the night before the crucifixion, Thomas had failed to comprehend the impending necessity of the Saviour's sacrifice; and when Jesus referred to going away and leaving the others to follow, Thomas asked how they could know the way. For his lack of understanding he stood reproved. He was absent when the resurrected Christ appeared to the assembled disciples in the evening of the day of His rising; and on being informed by the others that they had seen the Lord, he forcefully expressed his doubt, and declared he would not believe unless he could see and feel for himself the wounds in the crucified body. Eight days later the Lord visited the apostles again, when, as on the earlier occasion, they were within closed doors; and to Thomas the Lord said: "Reach hither thy finger, and behold my hands; and reach hither thy hand, and thrust it into my side." Then Thomas, no longer doubting but with love and reverence filling his soul, exclaimed "My Lord and my God." The Lord said unto him: "Thomas, because thou hast seen me, thou hast believed: blessed are they that have not seen, and yet have believed." Of Thomas no further record appears in the New

Testament aside from that of his presence with his fellows after the ascension.

James, son of Alpheus, is mentioned in the Gospels only in the matter of his ordination to the apostleship; and but once elsewhere in the New Testament by the appellation "Son of Alpheus." In writings other than scriptural he is sometimes designated as James II to avoid confusing him with James the son of Zebedee. There is acknowledged uncertainty concerning the identity of James the son of Alpheus as the James or one of the James's referred to in the Acts and the Epistles; and a plenitude of controversial literature on the subject is extant.

Judas is called Lebbeus Thaddeus by Matthew, Thaddeus by Mark, and Judas the brother of James by Luke. The only other specific reference to this apostle is made by John, and is incident to the last long interview between Jesus and the apostles, when this Judas, "not Iscariot," asked how or why Jesus would manifest Himself to His chosen servants and not to the world at large. The man's question shows that the really distinguishing character of the apostleship was not fully comprehended by him at that time.

Simon Zelotes, so designated in Acts, and as Simon called Zelotes in Luke's Gospel, is distinguished by both Matthew and Mark as the Canaanite. The last designation has no reference to the town of Cana, nor to the land of Canaan, neither is it in any sense of geographical signification; it is the Syro-Chaldaic equivalent of the Greek word which is rendered in the English translation "Zelotes." The two names, therefore, have the same fundamental meaning, and each refers to the Zealots, a Jewish sect or faction, known for its zeal in maintaining the Mosaic ritual. Doubtless Simon had learned moderation and toleration from the teachings of Christ; otherwise he would scarcely have been suited to the apostolic ministry. His zealous earnestness, properly directed, may have developed into a most serviceable trait of character. This apostle is nowhere in the scriptures named apart from his colleagues.

Judas Iscariot is the only Judean named among the Twelve; all the others were Galileans. He is generally understood to have been a resident of Kerioth, a small town in the southerly part of Judea, but a few miles west from the Dead Sea, though for this tradition, as also for the signification of his surname, we lack direct authority. So too we are uninformed as to his lineage, except that his father's name was Simon. He served as treasurer or agent of the apostolic company, receiving and disbursing such offerings as were made by disciples and friends, and purchasing supplies as required. That he was unprincipled and dishonest in the discharge of this trust is attested by John. His avaricious and complaining nature revealed itself in his murmuring against what he called a waste of costly spikenard, in the anointing of the Lord by Mary but a few days before the crucifixion; he hypocritically suggested that the precious ointment could have been sold and the proceeds given to the poor. The crowning deed of perfidy in the career of Iscariot was his deliberate betrayal of his Master to death; and this the infamous creature did for a price, and accomplished the foul deed with a kiss. He brought his guilty life to a close by a revolting suicide and his spirit went to the awful fate reserved for the sons of perdition.

General Characteristics of the Twelve

A survey of the general characteristics and qualifications of this body of twelve men reveals some interesting facts. Before their selection as apostles they had all become close disciples of the Lord; they believed in Him; several of them, possibly all, had openly confessed that He was the Son of God; and yet it is doubtful that any one of them fully understood the real significance of the Saviour's work. It is evident by the later remarks of many of them, and by the instructions and rebuke they called forth from the Master, that the common Jewish expectation of a Messiah who would reign in splendour as an earthly sovereign after He had subdued all other nations, had a place even in the hearts of these chosen ones. After long experience, Peter's concern was: "Behold, we have forsaken all, and followed thee; what shall we have therefore? They were as children to be trained and taught; but they were mostly willing pupils, receptive of soul, and imbued with a sincere eagerness to serve. To Jesus they were His little ones, His children, His servants, and His friends, as they merited. They were all of the common people, not rabbis, scholars, nor priestly officials. Their inner natures, not their outward accomplishments, were taken into prime account in the Lord's choosing. The Master chose them; they did not choose themselves; by Him they were ordained, and they could in consequence rely the more implicitly upon His guidance and support. To them much was given; much of them was required. With the one black exception they all became shining lights in the kingdom of God, and vindicated the Master's selection. He recognized in each the characteristics of fitness developed in the primeval world of spirits.

Disciples and Apostles

Discipleship is general; any follower of a man or devotee to a principle may be called a disciple. The Holy Apostleship is an office and calling belonging to the Higher or Melchizedek Priesthood, at once exalted and specific, comprising as a distinguishing function that of personal and special witness to the divinity of Jesus Christ as the one and only Redeemer and Saviour of mankind. The apostleship is an individual bestowal, and as such is conferred only through ordination. That the Twelve did constitute a council or "quorum" having authority in the Church established by Jesus Christ is shown by their ministrations after the Lord's resurrection and ascension. Their first official act was that of filling the vacancy in their organization occasioned by the apostasy and death of Judas Iscariot; and in connection with this procedure, the presiding apostle, Peter, set forth the essential qualifications of the one who would be chosen and ordained, which comprised such knowledge of Jesus, His life, death, and resurrection, as would make the new apostle one with the Eleven as special witnesses of the Lord's work. The ordination of the Twelve Apostles marked the inauguration of an advanced epoch in the earthly ministry of Jesus, an epoch characterized by the organization of a body of men invested with the authority of the Holy Priesthood, upon whom would rest, more particularly after the Lord's departure, the duty and responsibility of continuing the work He had begun, and of building up the Church established by Him.

The word "apostle" is an Anglicized form derived from the Greek apostolic, meaning literally "one who is sent," and connoting an envoy or official messenger, who speaks and acts by the authority of one superior to himself. In this sense Paul afterward applied the title to Christ as one specially sent and commissioned of the Father.

The Lord's purpose in choosing and ordaining the Twelve is thus enunciated by Mark: "And he ordained twelve, that they should be with him, and that he might send them forth to preach, and to have power to heal sicknesses, and to cast out devils." For a season following their ordination the apostles remained with Jesus, being specially trained and instructed by Him for the work then before them; afterward they were specifically charged and sent forth to preach and to administer in the authority of their priesthood, as shall be hereafter considered.

1. Judas Lubbers Thaddeus. This Judas not Iscariot is designated in the authorized version of Luke 6:16, and Acts 1:13, as "the brother of James." That the words "the brother" are an addition to the original text is indicated by italics. The revised version of these passages reads in each instance "the son of James," with italics of corresponding significance. The original reads "Judas of James." We are uninformed as to which James is referred to, and as to whether the Judas here mentioned was the son, the brother, or some other relative of the unidentified James.

2. The Meaning of Apostle. The title 'Apostle' is likewise one of special significance and sanctity; it has been given of God, and belongs only to those who have been called and ordained as 'special witnesses of the name of Christ in the entire world, thus differing from other officers in the Church in the duties of their calling. By derivation the word 'apostle' is the English equivalent of the Greek apostolos, indicating a messenger, an ambassador, or literally 'one who is sent.' It signifies that he who is rightly so called, speaks and acts not of himself, but as the representative of a higher power whence his commission issued; and in this sense the title is that of a servant,

rather than that of a superior. Even the Christ, however, is called an Apostle with reference to His ministry in the flesh Hebrews 3:1, and this appellation is justified by His repeated declaration that He came to earth to do not His own will but that of the Father by whom He was sent.

Though an apostle is thus seen to be essentially an envoy, or ambassador, his authority is great, as is also the responsibility associated therewith, for he speaks in the name of a power greater than his own the name of Him whose special witness he is. When one of the Twelve is sent to minister in any stake, mission or other division of the Church, or to labour in regions where no Church organization has been effected, he acts as the representative of the First Presidency, and has the right to use his authority in doing whatever is requisite for the furtherance of the work of God. His duty is to preach the Gospel, administer the ordinances thereof, and set in order the affairs of the Church, wherever he is sent. So great is the sanctity of this special calling, that the title 'Apostle' should not be used lightly as the common or ordinary form of address applied to living men called to this office. The quorum or council of the Twelve Apostles as existent in the Church today may better be spoken of as the 'Quorum of the Twelve,' the 'Council of the Twelve,' or simply as the 'Twelve,' than as the 'Twelve Apostles,' except as particular occasion may warrant the use of the more sacred term. It is advised that the title 'Apostle' be not applied as a prefix to the name of any member of the Council of the Twelve; but that such a one be addressed or spoken of as Elder and when necessary or desirable, as in announcing his presence in a public assembly, an explanatory clause may be added, thus, Elder one of the Council of the Twelve.

3. Of Alpheus, Son of Alpheus. In all Bible passages specifying "James son of Alpheus Matthew 10:3; Mark 3:18; Luke 6:15; Acts 1:13 the word son has been supplied by the translators, and therefore properly appears in italics. The phrase in the Greek reads "James of Alpheus." This fact must not be given undue weight in support of the thought

that the James spoken of was not the son of Alpheus; for the word son has been similarly added in the translation of other passages, in all of which italics are used to indicate the words supplied, e.g. "James the son of Zebedee Matthew 10:2; Mark 3:17.

Jesus is coming back as Lion of Judah and not the Lamb of God

Then one of the elders said to me, "Do not weep! See, the Lion of the tribe of Judah, the Root of David, has triumphed. He is able to open the scroll and its seven seals. John 1:29 Look, the Lamb of God, who takes away the sin of the world"

Rev 5:6 Then I saw a Lamb, looking as if it had been slain, standing in the centre of the throne.

And why is He called the Lion of Judah?

Revelation 5: 5 Then one of the elders said to me "Do not weep! See, the LION of the tribe of Judah, the root of David, has triumphed. He is able to open the scroll and its seven seals".

A. The phrase Lamb of God is a reference to the Passover lamb whose shed blood saved God's people from death and freed them from their bondage to slavery in Egypt **Exodus 12:12-13**.

Paul called Jesus our Passover Lamb in **1 Cor. 5:7**, and John the Baptist introduced Jesus as *the Lamb of God who takes away the sin of the world* **John 1:29**. He was saying that as the Passover lamb

THE LION OF JUDAH

redeemed the Jews from their bondage to slavery, the Lamb of God redeems us from our bondage to sin.

Lion of Judah comes from **Genesis 49:9-12** where Jacob called his son Judah a lion's cub, and prophesied that the Messiah would come from the tribe of Judah and be the ruler over the nations. That makes Lion of Judah a Messianic title and since Jesus is the Messiah who will rule the world, He is the Lion of Judah. Therefore The Lamb of God is a title associated with the Lord's first Coming, while the Lion of Judah points to His second coming.

In your book Understanding Revelation you explain predestination very nicely. It got me to thinking about all that and it made me wonder if the list of names in the Lambs Book of Life is the full number of believers. Would the full number be complete when the last person in the book believes?

A. Yes, I believe that the list of names in the Lamb's Book of Life was written before the foundation of the world was laid and constitutes the full number of Gentiles mentioned by Paul in **Romans 11:25**, and when the last name in the book is saved the Church will be complete and the rapture will occur.

In **Romans 8:29** Paul said, *For those God foreknew He also predestined to be conformed to the likeness of His Son.* To me this means God knew the names of everyone who would choose to become a believer before time and reserved a place for him or her in the Kingdom at that time

Very where we look we find people with concerns about the future. While we live in a world where knowledge is exploding, world events and growing uncertainty about tomorrow entice many who do not know God to pursue extraordinary and unusual means to do evil. Unable to find the answers that only God can give about tomorrow, they turn to psychics and those who make merchandise of their insight into the future. The Word of God promises, however, that believers can look toward tomorrow with expectation and excitement. Many of the answers we seek regarding future events are revealed in Bible prophecy. The Word of God declares: Shall a trumpet be blown in the city, and the people not are afraid? Shall there be evil in a city, and the LORD hath not done it? Surely the Lord GOD will do nothing, but he revealed his secret unto his servants the prophets Amos 3:6-7. Only God knows what tomorrow holds. But the Scriptures provide a glimpse into what lies ahead for those who know God Almighty. As we study His written Word and seek Him with our whole heart, He will reveal the secrets of tomorrow: But of that day and hour knoweth no man, no, not the angels of heaven, but my Father only Matthew 24:36.

We are told to be watchful: But know this that if the Goodman of the house had known in what watch the thief would come, he would have watched, and would not have suffered his house to be broken up. Therefore are ye also ready: for in such an hour as ye think not the Son of man cometh Matthew 24:43-44.

We are also cautioned to be aware of the times and seasons:

But of the times and the seasons, brethren, ye have no need that I write unto you. For yourselves know perfectly that the day of the Lord so cometh as a thief in the night. For when they shall say, Peace and safety; then sudden destruction cometh upon them, as travail upon a woman with child; and they shall not escape. But ye, brethren, are not in darkness, that that day should overtake you as a thief. 1 Thessalonians 5:1-4

As I consider world events and look at what is happening in the Holy Land, we must be aware of these perilous times as Bible prophecy rapidly unfolds before our eyes. We are living in a historic hour foretold by the prophets of old.

Prophetic Signs of the Times

As we study the Word of God, we discover five prophetic events that must occur before the coming of the Lord.

1. The Restoration of the State of Israel The Bible recognizes this restoration as the first event that must take place before the coming of the Lord:

Therefore, behold, the days come, said the LORD, that it shall no more be said, The LORD lives, that brought up the children of Israel out of the land of Egypt; But, The LORD live, that brought up the children of Israel from the land of the north, and from all the lands whither he had driven them: and I will bring them again into their land that I gave unto their fathers. Jeremiah 16:14-15

On May 14, 1948, Israel declared independence and proclaimed itself the State of Israel. Today, Jewish people from nations all over the world continue to return to their homeland. Bible prophecy also states that when the people return to their land, they will go back speaking the same language they spoke when they left: Thus said the LORD of hosts, the God of Israel; As yet they shall use this speech in the land of Judah and in the cities thereof, when I shall bring again their captivity; The LORD bless thee, O habitation of justice, and mountain of holiness Jeremiah 31:23. The nation of Israel had been scattered for 2,000 years. During those two centuries, the Jewish people retained their native tongue, even though they did not live in their land. With the restoration of Israel came the restoration of a people that were nearly eliminated from the face of the earth. But God Almighty said it is impossible to destroy them, for if you could destroy them, you would have to destroy the heavens first Jeremiah. 31:35, 37.

The restoration of Israel will bring about the fulfilment of all end-time prophecy, for Israel is God's time clock. Whatever happens in Israel affects the world. When the Most High divided to the nations their inheritance when he separated the sons of Adam he set the bounds of the people according to the number of the children of Israel Deuteronomy 32:8.

How should we understand the Lion and the Lamb passage?

Answer: Typically, when someone is thinking of the lion and the lamb, Isaiah 11:6 is in mind due to it often being misquoted, And the wolf will dwell with the lamb, and the leopard will lie down with the young goat, and the calf and the young lion and the fatling together. The true Lion and the Lamb passage is Revelation 5:5–6. The Lion and the Lamb both refer to Jesus Christ. He is both the conquering Lion of the tribe of Judah and the Lamb who was slain. The Lion and the Lamb are descriptions of two aspects of the nature of Christ. As the Lion of Judah, He fulfils the prophecy of Genesis 49:9 and is the Messiah who would come from the tribe of Judah. As the Lamb of God, He is the perfect and ultimate sacrifice for sin.

The scene of Revelation 4-5 is the heavenly throne room. After receiving the command to write to the seven churches in Asia Minor, John is caught up in the spirit to the throne room in heaven where he is to receive a series of visions that culminate in the ultimate victory of Christ at the end of the age. Revelation 4 shows us the endless praise that God receives from the angels and the 24 elders. Chapter 5 begins with John noticing that there is a scroll in the right hand of him who was seated on the throne. The scroll has writing on the inside and is sealed with seven seals. After giving us a description of the scroll, an angel proclaims with a loud voice, who is worthy to open the scroll and break its seals? John begins to despair when no one comes forth to answer the angel's challenge. One of the 24 elders encourages John to weep no more, and points out that the Lion of the tribe of Judah has come to take and open the scroll. The Lion of the tribe of Judah is obviously a reference to Christ. The image of the lion is meant to convey kingship. Jesus is worthy to receive and open the scroll because he is the King of God's people. Back in Genesis 49:9, when Jacob was blessing his sons, Judah is referred to as a lion's cub, and in verse 10 we learn that the sceptre shall not depart from Judah. The sceptre is a symbol of lordship and power. This was a prophecy that in Israel the kingly line would be descended from Judah. That prophecy was fulfilled when David succeeded to the throne after the death of King Saul 2 Samuel. David was descended from the line of Judah, and his descendants were the kings in Israel in Judah until the time of the Babylonian captivity in 586 BC.

This imagery of kingship is further enhanced when Jesus is described as the root of David. This harkens us back to the words of Isaiah the prophet: There shall come forth a shoot from the stump of Jesse, and a branch from his roots shall bear fruit. In that day the root of Jesse, who shall stand as a signal for the peoples of him shall the nations inquire, and his resting place shall be glorious Isaiah 11:1, 10. As the root of David, Jesus is not only being identified as a descendant of David, but also the source or root of David's kingly power.

Why is Jesus worthy to open the scroll? He is worthy because He has conquered. We know that, when Jesus returns, He will conquer all of God's enemies, as graphically described in Revelation 19. However, more importantly, Jesus is worthy because He has conquered sin and death at the cross. The cross was the ultimate victory of God over the forces of sin and evil. The events that occur at the return of Christ are the mop-up job to finish what was started at the cross. Because Jesus secured the ultimate victory at Calvary, He is worthy to receive and open the scroll, which contains the righteous judgment of God.

THE LION OF JUDAH

Christ's victory at the cross is symbolized by his appearance as a Lamb standing, as though it had been slain Revelation 5:6. Prior to the exodus from Egypt, the Israelites were commanded by God to take an unblemished lamb, slay it, and smear its blood on the doorposts of their homes Exodus 12:1–7. The blood of the slain lamb would set apart the people of Israel from the people of Egypt when the death angel came during the night to slay the firstborn of the land. Those who had the blood of the lamb would be spared. Fast forward to the days of John the Baptist. When he sees Jesus approaching him, he declares to all present, "Behold, the Lamb of God, who takes away the sin of the world!" John 1:29. Jesus is the ultimate Passover lamb who saves His people from eternal death. Nobody can say with any degree of certainty when Jesus is coming again, because He said clearly that even the angels in heaven do not know that day (see Mark 13:32). No man knows that day, and the Son of God, when He was on the earth, did not know either. This knowledge, the Lord Jesus said, was strictly reserved for the Father.

We can see certain signs, or clues (see Matthew 24:3, Luke 21:7), that His coming is approaching. Jesus said there would be wars and rumors of wars, revolutions, widespread famine, disease, and earthquakes in many different places (see Matthew 24:6-7, Luke 21:10-11). There would be an increase of lawlessness and anarchy. The apostle Paul said, "That day will not come unless the falling away comes first, and the man of sin is revealed, the son of perdition, who opposes and exalts himself above all that is called.

Another event that had to happen **before Jesus could return** was the **re-establishment of the state of Israel**. The original Israel disappeared from the globe hundreds of years ago. In 1948 a new state of Israel was established. The regathering of Jews to Israel is a clear sign, in both the Old and New Testaments, that **our age is just about over**. Jesus said, "Jerusalem will be trampled by Gentiles until the times of the Gentiles are fulfilled" (Luke 21:24). On June 6, 1967, the Jews, for the first time since Jerusalem was captured by Nebuchadnezzar in 586 B.C took over control of the entire city of Jerusalem, thus signalling the approaching end of Gentile world power.

Jesus said, however, that the one major thing which would herald His coming would be the proclamation of the gospel. He said, "This gospel of the kingdom will be preached in all the world as a witness to all the nations, and then the end will come" (Matthew 24:14).

These are **signs of the times**. We are to hold ourselves always **ready for our Lord's return**. But **nobody knows the day and hour** when that will be.

What Else Must Happen Before Christ Returns?

Some people teach that Jesus could come at any time because Jesus warned His disciples always to be watchful. While it is true that we do not know exactly when He will come, certain **signs of His coming** are given to us.

Jesus said **the coming of the Son of Man** will be just like the days of Noah (Matthew 24:37-39).

The thing that strikes me about the days of Noah is that even in the midst of te

This world will not end by a world war, an asteroid, a virus, a natural disaster, a man-made disaster, or any of the other typical events people imagine. And it's not that some (or even all) of these things won't occur between now and the time of the End, and be extremely devastating to life on the planet, even significantly reducing the Earth's population by their cumulative effects. It's just that these types of events will not cease ALL human life on the planet. No, this world will only end in one way - when Jesus returns to get His own, the Saved, away from it. Between now and then, by man's own choosing, the world will continue to get worse and worse in sin until there is finally no one else who will repent and come to God in Faith to be Saved.

"And as it was in the days of Noah, so it will be also in the days of the Son of Man: They ate, they drank, they married wives, they were given in marriage, until the day that Noah entered the ark, and the flood came and destroyed them all. Likewise as it was also in the days of Lot: They ate, they drank, they bought, they sold, they planted, they built; but on the day that Lot went out of Sodom it rained fire and brimstone from heaven and destroyed them all. Even so will it be in the day when the Son of Man is revealed. Jesus in Luke 17:26-30 (NKJV)

And so it is that prior to Jesus' Return, the world will again be as it was in the days of Noah. Yes, the people of the world at that time ate and drank and married, but their destruction was brought about by their spiritual condition that also reflected in the rest of their behavior, which is clearly defined in the Bible as the reason for the Flood: "Then the Lord saw that the wickedness of man was great in the earth, and that every intent of the thoughts of his heart was only evil continually." - Genesis 6:5 (NKJV)

This present world might not have <u>fully</u> returned to that same spiritual condition yet, but anyone can see that as bad continues to outweigh and outpace the good almost everywhere around the Earth, this world gets closer by the day.

It's not that sin didn't exist throughout history; it did. But even amidst the sinful world, there was always a remnant of True Believers in God's Word who were receptive to God's Way in Spirit and in Truth, as shown by their changed lives. After all, True Believers repent of sin and no longer contribute to its increase in the world. (They are not like the many hypocrites who say "Lord, Lord" and continue to practice lawlessness.)

True Believers also share God's Word of Love and Truth in a trustworthy manner with others, of whom a small number become New Believers, who mature into True Believers, thus continuing the cycle which, since the time of Noah, has always assured there are still some on the Earth who are willing to be Saved.

But the always-small stream of New Believers gradually reduces as the sin in the world increases.

Even so, since Noah, the sin of the world, while much, was not far-reaching enough to overwhelm the entire Earth where people lived and completely deplete the New Believer stream. And occasionally, small pockets of Revival even helped to replenish it. There was always at least some New Life somewhere in the world.

But starting a couple of centuries ago and continuing up through the present day, new technologies used in ways that have not been beneficial to human life have instead enabled such an overwhelming volume and degree of sin to persistently reach into almost every place on the Earth where people live that we are now past the point of no return.

Yes, there will be some New Believers here or there, in this place or that, until the End. But while they may be Saved, their number will not counteract sin's inertia in this present world, or the overall trend of decline in the New Believer stream until it is completely gone.

Again, we are talking about New Believers who become True Believers... those who give up wilful sin by worshipping God in the Truth. They are few. We are not talking about the multitude of others who follow the existing "beast" church to perdition, along with its harlot daughter churches who never really left the mother harlot. She can be spotted by comparing her commandments-of-men to God's Commandments, and noticing she has attempted to change the times and Law, specifically Commandments 2, 4, 9, and 10. She can also be spotted by her many other adulteries if one is willing to get a Real Bible (not hers) and actually read it, beginning with the Four Gospels of Jesus Christ - Matthew, Mark, Luke, and John - and comparing what Jesus says to what a church actually does, starting with the costumes their leaders wear, the titles with which they refer to themselves, and the fact that no man stands in God's or Jesus' place on the Earth. In this sinful, adulterous, and blasphemous world, it is no exaggeration to say that the devil's "false image" of Christianity is the extreme vast majority of it, while True Christianity - consisting of those who keep the Commandments of God and the Faith of Jesus Christ (Revelation 14:12) - is a tiny minority of it. It is not God's Will that so few are His and so many "worship the beast"; it's the choice of those who choose image over substance... the vast majority who find it easier to speak a lie than to live in the Truth.)

So, we are now past the tipping point, and it is just a matter of time until the End, which is prophesied.

But truly, what did we expect would happen?

Has no one noticed that as people, businesses, and nations have misused new technologies in sinful ways, such choices have only quickened the spread of selfishness; covetousness; greed; pride; self-exaltation; self-righteousness; disrespect; lies; slander; thefts; adulteries; lewdness; perversions; hatred; violence; murders; blasphemies; dishonour of family structures; abuse of God's True Sabbath; abuse of God's Name; and every form of lust, immaturity, and idolatry, including worship of money, people, culture, and self?

Has no one noticed the corresponding increase in thanklessness to God for giving us our lives, our Earth, our daily bread, our free will and power of choice to not only cease wilful sin but to choose well instead, and to also be forgiven of our sins through His Son, Jesus Christ, whom He also gave to us?

And if we say we have noticed the many sins of the world, have we hypocritically noticed only in regard to "other people or have we ourselves repented and turned from all such sin by Love for God and others?

Again, what should the world expect as the Creator's Will has been continually ignored, and even hated? It's not too hard to know. We reap what we sow, and increasing amounts of it. For they have sown the wind, and they shall reap the whirlwind..." - Hosea 8:7

And as the bad things increase, the good things - Faith, repentance, forgiveness, Love, mercy, kindness, humility, decency, modesty, wisdom, patience, self-control, perseverance, selflessness, respect, sharing, honesty, cooperation, good health, justice, peace, knowledge of Truth, an

At that time the sign of the Son of Man will appear in the sky, and all the nations of the earth will mourn. They will see the Son of Man coming on the clouds of the sky, with power and great glory Matthew 24:30.

This verse describes the literal return of Christ to the earth. The people of the earth will mourn when they see Christ returning because 1 they know he is coming in judgment, and 2 they will realize they are not ready for his coming. This will be a sign visible to the entire earth. Behold, he is coming with the clouds, and every eye will see him, even those who pierced him, and all tribes of the earth will wail on account of him Revelation 1:7.

The Second Coming of Christ will be with power and great glory. Perhaps the best way to understand that statement is to compare the circumstances surrounding the first and second comings. The first time Jesus came unnoticed into the world, the second time "every eye will see him." In his first coming Jesus humbled himself, being born in a stable in Bethlehem. When he returns, he will come back as King of Kings and Lord of Lords. In his first coming he endured the mockery of men who despised him for his goodness. Although he was the Son of God, he allowed them to put him to death, that he might thereby provide salvation for the world. When he comes again, all mockery will cease for he will rule the nations with a rod of iron. He came the first time as the Lamb of God; he comes again as

THE LION OF JUDAH

the Lion of the Tribe of Judah. Two thousand years ago the religious leaders shouted in scorn, "He saved others, but he can't save himself!" (Matthew 24:42). The day is coming when the whole world will see Jesus as he really is. When that happens, every knee will bow and every tongue confess that Jesus Christ is Lord, to the glory of God the Father (Philippians 2:9-11)

Around the first coming inscribe the word *HUMILTY* in letters large and bold. Around His second coming inscribe the word *GLORY* so that all the world may see. Nothing could be more natural than a triumphant return of our victorious Lord. Though He was once "despised and rejected of men," He will one day return "in power and great glory," heralded by angels and accompanied by his saints.

These facts from biblical prophecy about Christ's return may surprise you:

- One out of every 30 verses in the Bible mentions the subject of Christ's return or the end of time.
- Of the 216 chapters in the New Testament, there are well over 300 references to the return of Christ.
- 23 of the 27 New Testament books mention Christ's return.
- In the Old Testament, such well-known and reliable men of God as Job, Moses, David, Isaiah, Jeremiah, Daniel, as well as most of the Minor Prophets mention Christ's return in their writings.
- Christ often spoke specifically about His own return to earth.
- Throughout the centuries, Christ's disciples and followers have adamantly believed, written, and taught that Christ would someday return to earth.

The Bible teaches it. The Lord Jesus stood upon its truths. The apostles declared it and wrote about it. The creeds include it and affirm it.

Quite obviously, His return has not been considered an insignificant issue through the centuries. But the strange thing is that many Christians in this generation either ignore it or are somehow confused by it. Too bad. It is a marvellous truth.

The lighting cannot strike without dark clouds.

Jesus have told us that there will be horrible times on Earth, just before His return. The end of this age will be ruled by deception, false teachings and people giving other's prophecies out of their imagination.

Once I was invited to a YWAM base for a seminar where *"teachers"* were going to teach us how to become prophets. I washed the dust off my feet, and left.

God of the Bible, Father, Son and Spirit, has appeared as lightening many times in the Old Testament. Almost without exception as a strike of judgment and punishment.

Exodus 9:23

When Moses stretched out his staff toward the sky, the LORD sent thunder and hail, and lightning flashed down to the ground. So the LORD rained hail on the land of Egypt;

2 Samuel 22:15

He shot arrows and scattered the enemies, bolts of lightning and routed them.

Job 37:11

He loads the clouds with moisture; he scatters his lightning through them.

In Ezekiel we read about a vision of God, that materialize Himself in flashes of lightening.

THE LION OF JUDAH

Ezekiel 1:13

The appearance of the living creatures was like burning coals of fire or like torches. Fire moved back and forth among the creatures; it was bright, and lightning flashed out of it.

Daniel saw a body, with a face light lightening.

Daniel 10:6

His body was like chrysolite, his face like lightning, his eyes like flaming torches, his arms and legs like the gleam of burnished bronze, and his voice like the sound of a multitude.

The Messiah has appeared many times, not in flesh. But in the form of lightening. In this way, the Pagan Vikings was not totally of the mark. But instead of recognizing the Creator, they started to worship the lightening.

Rapture and lightening. Tools used by our living God, Jesus of Nazareth.

Hosea 6:5

Therefore I cut you in pieces with my prophets, I killed you with the words of my mouth; my judgments flashed like lightning upon you.

The Old Testament prophet Zechariah has foretold that the Messiah will return in flashes of Lightening.

Zechariah 9:14 The LORD Will Appear Then the LORD will appear over them; his arrow will flash like lightning. The Sovereign LORD will sound the trumpet; he will march in the storms of the south.

I believe Jesus is returning to reign on earth because the Old Testament prophets say so.

Psalm 2:6-9 David says the Messiah will reign over the very ends of the earth from Mount Zion in Jerusalem.

Psalm 22:27-31 David again affirms that the Messiah will be given dominion over the ends of the earth at the time when He rules over the nations.

Psalm 47 The sons of Korah rejoice over the day when the Lord will be a great King over all the earth, and they state that this will take place when the Lord subdues the nations under our feet.

Psalm 67 an unidentified psalmist speaks prophetically of the time when the nations of the world will be glad and sing for joy. This will be when the Lord comes to judge the peoples with uprightness. At that time the Lord will guide the nations on the earth so that all the ends of the earth may fear Him.

Psalm 89:19-29 The psalmist, Ethan, speaks of the Davidic Covenant and proclaims that it will be fulfilled when God makes His first-born the highest of the kings of the earth.

Psalm 110 David said a time will come when God will make the enemies of the Messiah a footstool under His feet. This will occur when the Messiah stretches forth His strong scepter from Zion. At that time He will rule in the midst of His enemies, for He will shatter kings in the day of His wrath, He will judge among the nations.

Psalm 132:13-18 An unnamed psalmist speaks of God's fulfilment of the Davidic Covenant. He said this will occur at a time when the horn of David springs forth to reign from Zion. He says His crown will shine, and He will make Zion His resting place forever for He will dwell there.

Isaiah 2:1-4 Isaiah said that in the last days the Messiah will reign from Mount Zion in Jerusalem and the entire world will experience peace.

Isaiah 9:6-7 The Messiah will rule from the throne of David, giving the world a government of peace, justice, and righteousness. Note: The throne of David is not in Heaven. It is located in Jerusalem Psalm 122. Jesus is not now on the throne of David. He sits at the right hand of His Father on His Father's throne se Revelation 3:21.

Isaiah 11:3b-9 The Messiah will bring righteousness and fairness to the earth when He returns to slay the wicked. At that time, the curse will be lifted and the plant and animal kingdoms will be restored to their original perfection.

Isaiah 24:21-23 When the Messiah returns, He will punish Satan and his demonic hordes in the heavens and then will punish the kings of the earth, on earth. He will then reign on Mount Zion and in Jerusalem for the purpose of manifesting His glory.

Jeremiah 23:5 Behold, the days are coming,' declares the Lord, when I shall raise up for David a righteous Branch; and He will reign as king and act wisely and do justice and righteousness in the land.' Note: The term, Branch, is a Messianic title.

Jeremiah 33:6-18 A day will come when the Lord will gather the dispersed of both Judah and Israel and will save a great remnant. At that time the Lord will cause a righteous Branch of David to spring forth; and He shall execute justice and righteousness on the earth.

Ezekiel 20:33-44 The Lord says a day will come when He will gather the Jews to their land and will enter into judgment with them. He says that at that time "I shall be king over you." He then adds that "the whole house of Israel, all of them, will serve Me in the land."

Ezekiel 37:24-28 The Lord says that He will dwell in the midst of Israel after a remnant of the Jews is gathered to the land and saved, and He promises that "David My servant shall be their prince forever."

Ezekiel 39:21-29 The Lord said that following the battle of Armageddon verses 17-20, I will set My glory among the nations;

and all the nations will see My judgment which I have executed, and My hand which I have laid on them.

Ezekiel 43:7 While being given a tour of the future Millennial Temple, Ezekiel is told by the Lord: Son of man, this is the place of My throne and the place of the soles of My feet; where I will dwell among the sons of Israel forever."

Daniel 7:13-14,18,27 Daniel says he was given a vision in which he saw the Messiah Son of Man given dominion over all the earth by God the Father the Ancient of Days. And then he adds in verses 18 and 27 that the kingdom is shared "with the saints of the Highest One," and they are allowed to exercise sovereignty with Him over "all the kingdoms under the whole heaven."

Hosea 3:4-5 — The Jews will be set aside "for many days," but a time will come "in the last days" when they "will return and seek the Lord their God and David their king."

Joel 3:14-17,21 Joel says that following the battle of Armageddon verses 14-16, the Lord will dwell in Zion, My holy mountain. He repeats this in verse 21. And in verse 17 He identifies Zion as the city of Jerusalem.

Micah 4:1-7 Micah repeats in greater detail the prophecy contained in Isaiah 2. Like Isaiah, he says the Lord will make Jerusalem the capital of the world. The world will be flooded with peace and prosperity. All believing Jews will be gathered to Israel, and the Lord will reign over them in Mount Zion."

Zephaniah 3:14-20 This entire book is devoted to a description of the day the Lord will return to the earth in vengeance. The prophet says that at the end of that day, when the Lord's enemies have been destroyed, the Jewish remnant will shout in triumphant joy because the King of Israel, the Lord, will be in their midst. Haggai 2:20-23 The Lord said that a day will come when He will overthrow the thrones of kingdoms and destroy the power of the kingdoms of the nations. Then, using Zerubbabel, governor of Judah, as a type of the Messiah, the prophet adds: On that day, declares the Lord of hosts, 'I will take you, Zerubbabel, son of Shealtiel, my servant,' declares the Lord, 'and I will make you like a signet ring, for I have chosen you,' declares the Lord of hosts." The reference to the signet ring means the Father will grant His Son ruling authority. Forty days after His Resurrection, Jesus and His Apostles were gathered together on the Mount of Olives. The time had come for Jesus to leave the earth. He had completed all the work that He had to do at that time. He was to return to our Heavenly Father until the time of His Second Coming.

After He had instructed His Apostles, Jesus ascended

The story of Daniel in the lion's den, recorded in Daniel 6, is one of the most beloved in all Scripture. Briefly, the story involves Daniel, a prophet of the true and living God, who defies King Darius's decree that the people should pray only to the Persian king for thirty days. Daniel, an otherwise law-abiding man, continues to pray to Israel's God as he has always done. Evil men, who instigated the decree in the first place in order to entrap Daniel, of whom they were jealous, report him to Darius. The king is forced to put Daniel into a den of lions where he would be torn to pieces. King Darius is greatly distressed about having to punish Daniel, and he says to Daniel, May your God, whom you serve continually, rescue you Daniel 6:16. God does indeed rescue Daniel, sending His angel to shut the mouths of the lions so they do not harm him. Daniel is removed from the lions' den the next day, much to the relief of the king. One of the chief lessons we learn from this narrative is gleaned from the confession of King Darius himself: For he is the living God and he endures forever; his kingdom will not be destroyed, his dominion will never end Daniel 6:26. For only by faith in such a God could any man have shut the mouths of lions Hebrews 11:33. As with Daniel, the faithful Christian must understand that God is sovereign and omnipotent and His will permeates and supersedes every aspect of life.

It is God's will that takes precedence over everything and everyone. The psalmist tells us, As for God, His way is perfect Psalm 18:30. If God's ways are perfect, then we can trust that whatever He does and whatever He allows is also perfect. This may not seem possible to us, but our minds are not God's mind. It is true that we can't expect to understand His mind perfectly, as He reminds us in Isaiah 55:8-9. Nevertheless, our responsibility to God is to obey Him, to trust Him, and to submit to His will and believe that whatever He ordains will be for our benefit and His glory Romans 8:28. In Daniel's case, "no wound was found on him, because he had trusted his God Daniel 6:23. Joseph, too, understood that sometimes evil men plan things for evil, but God means them for good Genesis 50:20.

There is more to learn from this remarkable story that makes it relevant to our postmodern culture. Peter tells us in 1 Peter 2:13-20 to submit yourselves for the Lord's sake to every authority instituted among men: whether to the king, as the supreme authority, or to governors, who are sent by him 1 Peter 2:13-14. Daniel not only followed this principle, he exceeded it by distinguishing himself as one with exceptional qualities Daniel 6:2-3. Taking this lesson further, we read that submission to our political authorities is God's will that by doing good you should silence the ignorant talk as foolish men 1 Peter 2:15. Daniel's faithfulness, his outstanding work ethic, and integrity made it next to impossible for his adversaries to find "grounds for charges against him Daniel 6:4. Instead, they found that he was trustworthy and neither corrupt nor negligent. The world now, as it did then, judges us not by our faith but by our conduct James 2:18. How many today could stand such a scrutiny as did Daniel on this occasion?

The story ends badly for Daniel's accusers, just as it will for those who accuse and persecute Christians today. King Darius, on the other hand, recognized the power of the God of Daniel, turned to Him in faith, and commanded the people of his kingdom to worship Him Daniel 6:25–27. Through the witness of Daniel, his faith, and the faithfulness and power of God, an entire nation came to know and reverence the Lord. For he is the living God and he endures forever; his kingdom will not be destroyed, his dominion will never end.

A friend of mine once remarked, A lot of crimes are not sins, and a lot of sins are not crimes. Our text indicates he was absolutely right. In the sixth chapter of Daniel, this righteous man is convicted of a crime which is not a sin. Daniel purposefully committed this crime because he did not wish to commit a sin, which was not a crime.

Daniel's deliverance from the lion's den, one of the most popular and well-known Bible stories, is not the first great deliverance in the Book of Daniel, but it is the best loved. Daniel and his three friends are divinely delivered in chapter 1 from a confrontation with the Babylonian government and Nebuchadnezzar its king. While these four godly Hebrews were willing to be called by Babylonian names, attend Babylonian schools, and even work for a Babylonian government, they were not willing to eat the food served at the king's table.

God granted these men favour in the eyes of their foreign superiors, and they were allowed to eat vegetables, rather than the food set aside for them by their king. Because of their faithfulness, God gave these men an extra measure of wisdom, greatly impressing king Nebuchadnezzar, who gave them positions of influence and responsibility in his kingdom.

In chapter 2, once again God delivered Daniel and his three friends. King Nebuchadnezzar had a dream he could not understand; neither could his counsellors and wise men reveal or interpret the dream. In anger, the king commanded the execution of all the wise men of the land, including Daniel and his friends. In the providence of God, Daniel learned of the king's dilemma and was able to reveal to the king his dream and its meaning, sparing his own life and the lives of the other Babylonian wise men.

In chapter 3, Nebuchadnezzar created a great golden image, before which the people of all nations were to bow in worship. Daniel's three friends refused to bow down. Again in anger, Nebuchadnezzar threatened them with death if they did not obey his decree. Refusing to obey, they were thrown into a fiery furnace. God was present with them there and preserved them from death, injury, and even the smell of fire. The king was so impressed he issued a decree guaranteeing the Jews freedom to worship their God without hindrance.

Chapter 4 speaks of Nebuchadnezzar's deliverance. He is delivered from his pride and oppression when, for a period, his sanity and kingdom are removed from him, and he must live like a beast of the field. From his own testimony, it appears he came to genuine repentance and saving faith as a result of God's working in his life.

Chapter 5 witnesses Belshazzar's condemnation in contrast to Nebuchadnezzar's conversion in chapter 4. Because of his rejection of the truth, and his blasphemy against the God of Israel, only one day in the life of Belshazzar is recorded in Scripture, only to announce his condemnation and death.

Now, in chapter 6, Daniel's life is in danger, and he will experience God's deliverance. Daniel 1 reveals what set Daniel apart from the rest of his Jewish peers and brought him to a position of prominence and power in king Nebuchadnezzar's administration. But chapter 6 identifies what sustained Daniel over the many years of his ministry and enabled him to survive the crises of his life.

While Daniel deservedly commands canter stage of our text, much can be learned from King Darius and even Daniel's peers, who seek to arrange his downfall and destruction. Once again in the Book of Daniel, we are reminded that God is able to deliver His people, even in a distant land. The inspired and inspiring words of our text have much to teach us.

Daniel in the Critics Den which was described by Two books which share the same title are entitled *Daniel in the Critics Den*. Correctly, two Christian authors have compared Daniel's experience in the lion's den to the critics' attack on the Book of Daniel itself. Chapter 6 is one of the portions under heaviest attack. A message as important and encouraging as that found in our text could be expected to come under attack.

The primary issue of chapter 6 is the identity of Darius. Secular history has no record of a king named Darius. We need no outside confirmation of reliability if we believe the Bible to be divinely inspired, accurate, and authoritative. If we reject the Bible's authority, historical confirmation of its teachings will certainly be insufficient to change minds. One explanation suggests Darius is simply another name for Cyrus, a view some respected evangelical scholars hold. Our previous text in chapter 5 indicated that until recent years, nothing was known of Belshazzar. In twenty or forty years, we may know as much about Darius as we now know about Belshazzar. We must not be distracted from the richness and the blessings of this chapter by the clamouring of the skeptics, who would not take this chapter seriously even if Darius were a well-known king. What truly offends the unbelieving mind is the claim of a miraculous divine deliverance, not the lack of historical evidence. God's miracles and moral standards are both offensive to fallen man.

The Conspiracy Daniel 6:1-9

It seemed good to Darius to appoint 120 satraps over the kingdom, that they should be in charge of the whole kingdom, and over them three commissioners of whom Daniel was one, that these satraps might be accountable to them, and that the king might not suffer loss. Then this Daniel began distinguishing himself among the commissioners and satraps because he possessed an extraordinary spirit, and the king planned to appoint him over the entire kingdom. Then the commissioners and satraps began trying to find a ground of accusation against Daniel in regard to government affairs; but they could find no ground of accusation or evidence of corruption, inasmuch as he was faithful, and no negligence or corruption was to be found in him. Then these men said, we shall not find any ground of accusation against this Daniel unless we find it against him with regard to the law of his God. Then these commissioners and satraps came by agreement to the king and spoke to him as follows: King Darius, live forever! All the commissioners of the kingdom, the prefects and the satraps, the high officials and the governors have consulted together that the king should establish a statute and enforce an injunction that anyone who makes a petition to any god or man besides you, O king, for thirty days, shall be cast into the lions' den. Now, O king, establish the injunction and sign the document so that it may not be changed, according to the law of the Medes and Persians, which may not be revoked. Therefore King Darius signed the document, that is, the injunction. Daniel 5 informs the reader of

Belshazzar's defeat and the end of the Babylonian kingdom, the head of gold of Daniel 2. The kingdom of the Medes and the Persians commences at the end of chapter 5, when Darius becomes the first king of this new empire at approximately 62 years of age Daniel 5:31

Chapter 6 accounts Daniel's rapid rise to power, the threat it posed to his peers, and ultimately to his own life. Verses 1-9 depict a sequence of events which give birth to a conspiracy against Daniel, leading to a law which makes Daniel a criminal and sentences him to the death penalty.

Darius may have been new at the task of ruling an empire, but he was far from naive. To establish himself and his rule over the territory formerly ruled by Babylon, he appoints 120 satraps, each responsible for a certain geographical region. The king's major concern was corruption. He knew that political power afforded the opportunity not only for oppression but for corruption. Darius feared he would not be able to adequately supervise the satraps with such a large kingdom, and they would enrich themselves at his expense. For this reason, the king appointed three governors over the one hundred and twenty satraps. He wanted to create a system of accountability which would prevent him from suffering loss. Darius may have become familiar with Daniel in a number of ways. It certainly appears unusual for this Hebrew, who had been so intimately associated with the Babylonian kingdom Darius had just overthrown, to rise so quickly to a position of power under this Mede. While the text does not say, we would hardly be wrong to conclude that, as before, God gave Daniel favour in the sight of this king.

Daniel's rise to power under Darius did not rest upon his remarkable accomplishments of the past. We are told Daniel began distinguishing himself among the commissioners and satraps because of the extraordinary spirit he possessed. I believe Darius recognized not only Daniel's wisdom but his integrity and faithfulness. Here was a man he could trust in a leadership position who would not cause him to suffer loss. Recognizing his unique abilities, Darius planned to promote Daniel, placing him in charge of all the commissioners and the satraps. The king's plan to promote Daniel seems to have become public knowledge; at least the commissioners and satraps knew. The thought of Daniel's promotion created much consternation.

This crisis must be taken most seriously. Why? What distressed them so greatly? The common view is that Daniel's peers were jealous. Perhaps so, but the matter seems more serious to them.

The context supplies the reason for their distress. His ability threatened them, but more so his honesty. The king was delighted to find a man of ability and honesty. To the corrupt leaders of the kingdom, Daniel's ability and honesty seriously threatened their corruption. They could neither corrupt Daniel nor deceive him. If he were to rise above them, they could not continue.

Daniel's testimony is awesome, his character and ability unsurpassed.

Then Jacob departed from Beersheba and went toward Haran. And he came to a certain place and spent the night there, because the sun had set; and he took one of the stones of the place and put it under his head, and lay down in that place. And he had a dream, and behold, a ladder was set on the earth with its top reaching to heaven; and behold, the angels of God were ascending and descending on it. And behold, the Lord stood above it and said, I am the Lord, the God of your father Abraham and the God of Isaac; the land on which you lie, I will give it to you and to your descendants. Your descendants shall also be like the dust of the earth, and you shall spread out to the west and to the east and to the north and to the south; and in you and in your descendants shall all the families of the earth be blessed. And behold, I am with you, and will keep you wherever you go, and will bring you back to this land; for I will not leave you until I have done what I have promised you. Then Jacob awoke from his sleep and said, "Surely the Lord is in this place, and I did not know it." And he was afraid and said, "How awesome is this place! This is none other than the house of God, and this is the gate of heaven Genesis 28:10-17.

But will God indeed dwell on the earth? Behold heaven and the highest heaven cannot contain Thee, how much less this house which I have built! Yet have regard to the prayer of Thy servant and to his supplication, O Lord my God, to listen to the cry and to the prayer which Thy servant prays before Thee today; that Thine eyes may be open toward this house night and day, toward the place of which Thou hast said, 'My name shall be there,' to listen to the prayer which Thy servant shall pray toward this place. And listen to the supplication of Thy servant and of Thy people Israel, when they pray toward this place; hear Thou in heaven Thy dwelling place; hear and forgive When they sin against Thee for there is no man who does not sin and Thou art angry with them and dost deliver them to an enemy, so that they take them away captive to the land of the enemy, far off or near; if they take thought in the land where they have been taken captive, and repent and make supplication to Thee in the land of those who have taken them captive, saying, We have sinned and have committed iniquity, we have acted wickedly' if they return to Thee with all their heart and with all their soul in the land of their enemies who have taken them captive, and pray to Thee toward their land which Thou hast given to their fathers, the city which Thou hast chosen, and the house which I have built for Thy name; then hear their prayer and their supplication in heaven Thy dwelling place, and maintain their cause, and forgive Thy people who have sinned against Thee and all their transgressions which they have transgressed against Thee, and make them objects of compassion before those who have taken them captive, that they may have compassion on them for they are Thy people and Thine inheritance which Thou hast brought forth from Egypt, from the midst of the iron furnace, that Thine eyes may be open to the supplication of Thy servant and to the supplication of Thy people Israel, to listen to them whenever they call to Thee. For Thou hast separated them from all the peoples of the earth as Thine inheritance, as Thou didst speak through Moses Thy servant, when Thou didst bring our fore fathers forth from Egypt, O Lord God 1 Kings 8:27-30, 46-53 and also 2 Chronicles 6:20-40.

There we sat down and wept, when we remembered Zion. Upon the willows in the midst of it we hung our harps. For there our captors demanded of us songs, And our tormentors mirth, saying, Sing us one of the songs of Zion. How can we sing the LORD'S song in a foreign land? If I forget you, O Jerusalem, May my right hand forget her skill. May my tongue cleave to the roof of my mouth, if I do not remember you, if I do not exalt Jerusalem Above my chief joy? Remember, O LORD, against the sons of Edom The day of Jerusalem, Who said, Raze it, raze it, To its very foundation. O daughter of Babylon, you devastated one, How blessed will be the one who repays you with the recompense with which you have repaid us, How blessed will be the one who seizes and dashes your little ones against the rock Psalm 137:1-9.

God made a promise to Abraham in Genesis 12:1-3 known as the Abrahamic covenant. In this covenant, God promised Abraham a land, a seed, and a blessing. Through Abraham, his seed, and his blessing, the nations too would be blessed. When Jacob left the Promised Land to flee from his brother and to seek a wife among his relatives, he had a vision of a ladder on which angels were ascending and descending. For the first time in his life, he was awe struck that this land of Canaan was a holy place. Even more, somehow it was a place of mediation, a place where heaven and earth met. The same truth is later affirmed by Solomon at the time of the dedication of the temple in Jerusalem. God's dwelling place was not the temple, Solomon confessed. Even the heavens were not able to contain God, much less a temple in Jerusalem. But Jerusalem was the place where God chose to meet with men and to bless them. Solomon spoke in his prayer of men praying toward Jerusalem, the place where God would meet with men to bless them. He specifically spoke of God's people praying toward Jerusalem from the lands where they were captives.

One such prayer recorded for us is Psalm 137. There, from Babylon, the psalmist cries out to the God of Israel. The eyes of the psalmist look toward Jerusalem and long to return there to worship God.

Jerusalem is in ruins, but the psalmist is not deterred from looking toward that city. It did motivate him to petition God to judge those who brought about the destruction of this city.

I believe Daniel consistently prayed toward Jerusalem three times a day for the more than seventy years of his sojourn in Babylon. Ironically, we can confidently assume that many of those prayers of petition were for the blessing of the king and kingdom of Babylon Jeremiah 7:13-17. The conspirators passed a law intended to prevent the very prayers which brought God's blessings on this nation and its people.

The Jewish captives brought the blessings of God on the kingdom of their captors. The city of Jerusalem not only symbolized the hopes of the Jews, but it is the place their God met with them and heard their prayers. God chose to mediate His blessings through His chosen people, the Jews, and through His chosen place Jerusalem.

While the king may not have thought through the implications of the injunction which he made law, Daniel did. The law passed by the conspirators in effect, made Darius the mediator between all gods and men. I do not believe the king was declaring himself to be god. Neither do I believe he put himself above all gods. But his injunction did make him the link between all those in his kingdom and any god.

Here the conflict between Daniel's faith as a Jew and the injunction of Darius became irresolvable. According to the new law, the king will be a mediator for 30 days. According to Daniel of his faith as Jewish Law of the Old Testament Scriptures, the God of Israel is God alone to be worship, and every blessing will be from his people Israel. Their petitions must be directed to God, but through the place of His blessing, Jerusalem. There was no way Daniel could redirect his petitions to the king, rather than to God, by facing Jerusalem he is assured that all his help will come from a place where God meet to give bless.

It does not seem possible for Daniel to pray to God, toward Jerusalem, other than by literally looking in that direction. This meant his window would be open and he would be visible when he prayed. He prayed publicly, in defiance of the law of the Medes and the Persians, because he believed there was no other supreme being than his God.

I can almost see the conspirators deciding how they will catch Daniel breaking their law. His prayer life was so consistent that they could literally pick the time to catch him praying but he knows that the only option for him to counter his evil conspirators is too appalled to his God for deliverance.

Jesus as Judge

John's gospel, Chapter 5, is very important to this entire discussion.

For the Father loves the Son, and shows Him all things that He Himself does and He will show Him greater works than these, that you may marvel. For as the Father raises the dead and gives life to them, even so the Son gives life to whom He will. For the Father judges no one, but has committed all judgment to the Son, that all should honour the Son just as they honour the Father. He who does not honour the Son does not honour the Father who sent Him. Most assuredly, I say to you, he who hears My word and believes in Him who sent me has giving him everlasting life, but shall not come into judgment, but has passed from death into life.

Most assuredly, I say to you, the hour is coming, and now is, when the dead will hear the voice of the Son of God and those who hear will live. For as the Father has life in Himself, so He has granted the Son to have life in Himself, and has given Him authority to execute judgment also, because He is the Son of Man.

Do not marvel at this; for the hour is coming in which all who are in the graves will hear His voice and come forth--those who have done good, to the resurrection of life, and those who have done evil, to the resurrection of condemnation.

I cannot of myself do anything. As I hear, I judge; and my judgment is righteous, because I do not seek my own will but the will of the Father who sent Me John 5: 20-30 Since God is both holy and just, He must judge evil and vindicate recompense those who have been wronged. He does this in accordance with His own time tables and calendar. In the Lamentations and of Jeremiah we learn that God's judgments are undertaken reluctantly after all else fails. God is slow to anger" and very patient and longsuffering, but when He does judge He is thorough and even to us ruthless.

The claim of Jesus is that life belongs to him. He only loans it, for a while, to us. Think of that! It cuts right across the philosophy and the propaganda of our day! Television, radio, newspapers and magazines tell you that your life belongs to you, and you can do with it what you want it is up to you to make of yourself whatever you desire. But that is a lie! Your life is not yours You did not invent it, you were handed it, you were given it. One of these days you will have to give it back. Those two great facts underscore all of life, yet how easy it is to forget them.

How frequently the world tries to operate on a basis that is not true, that life belongs to us, and it will go on as long as we want it to! One of the reasons we gather here Sunday after Sunday is that we might counteract that lie and remind ourselves afresh that many of the things that are being said to us by the world are not true, they are not based on reality. Sooner or later, an exciting, compelling, terrifying reality is going to crash in upon us and we will have to deal with life the way it really is. That is what this claim of Jesus states. He claims not only to possess the power to give physical life, but spiritual life as well. Spiritual life is what the Bible calls eternal life. It is a different level of life. It is not merely, as it is frequently translated especially in the King James Version everlasting life. That conveys the idea that this present, earthly life will be extended infinitely. But that is not what the Bible is talking about when it speaks of "spiritual" or "eternal" life. It is rather describing a quality of life. It is true that it goes on forever, but primarily the Bible is talking about the richness, the fullness, the beauty of life. It is a quality of life that is enduring, true, but it is also enriching; it cannot be diminished by circumstances or ended by death. It is a quality of life that is given to us now. It begins here, not in heaven after you die. The claim of Jesus is that he alone has the power to give that kind of life.

Because Jesus gives "to whom he will," that makes him also the arbiter of the destiny of human beings: He is the Judge of all men. It is his knowledge of who is to receive eternal life, and who is to remain without it, that constitutes him an infallible Judge of human destiny. These two ideas blend together; one grows out of the other. If Jesus gives you life you are on your way to heaven. If he gives you eternal life you will never die, you will never taste the emptiness and awful loneliness of death. You will immediately have a fuller experience of life than you have ever had before. But only if Jesus gives it to you. He is the sole possessor of spiritual life.

If he does not give your life then you remain exactly the way you were, on your way to hell, on your way to frustration, torment, hollowness all those negative things the Scripture means when it speaks of hell life without God, without blessing, without richness, without fullness.

If this claim of Jesus is, real it clearly makes him the most important Person in anybody's life. If your very physical existence has come from him, and your spiritual destiny is in his hands, then he is the most important Person you will ever have to deal with. More than that, he is the most important Person in the whole world, the central figure in the entire universe. This is stated all through the Scriptures.

In the last book of the Bible, which was also written by the Apostle John, there is a tremendous scene described in Chapter 5, where John takes us beyond the limits of earth and shows us the throne of God. The creatures of heaven are gathered around the throne, worshiping God, and in the centre of the scene John sees a Lamb that has been slain. Here is his description:

Then I looked, and I heard around the throne and the living creatures and the elders the voice of many angels, numbering myriads of myriads and thousands of thousands, and saying with a loud voice, "Worthy is the Lamb who was slain, to receive power and wealth and wisdom and might and honour and glory and blessing!" And I heard every creature in heaven and on earth and under the earth and in the sea, and all therein, saying, To him who sits upon the throne and to the Lamb be blessing and honour and glory and might for ever and ever! And the four living creatures said, Amen! and the elders fell down and worshiped. Rev 5:11-14

There is Jesus, sitting at the heart of the universe. Because of this, no Christian can ever put Jesus Christ on a par with Mohammed, Buddha, Mahatma Gandhi, the Virgin Mary, Moses, the prophets, or any religious leader of any time. This is why we cannot call a Christian one who only accepts the teachings of Jesus, or who adopts his moral standards, or admires him as a social reformer or religious leader. Jesus himself does not allow us that privilege. He is above all of this. He alone has the right to give the gift of eternal life. In his first letter, John has written of him, this is the record that God has given us eternal life, and this life is in his Son. He who has the Son has life, but he who does not have the Son of God does not have life, 1 John 5:11-12. The relationship you have to Jesus Christ is the most important relationship of your life. It determines your ultimate destiny.

If that is true, the great question before us is, To whom and on what terms does Jesus give eternal life? The answer to that is given in one of the greatest verses in Scripture, Verse 24. It is one of my favourite texts, one I have used many, many times. I hope you will memorize these words of Jesus,

Truly, truly, I say to you remember, that introduction in effect underlines the words that follow, calling attention to the importance of them, he who hears my word and believes him who sent me, has eternal life; he does not come into judgment, but has passed from death to life. John 5:24 RSV

That verse makes clear that when Jesus says he gives life to which he will, it is not a matter of arbitrary selection on his part. He does not point at people in a capricious way, and say, You, and you, and you, can have eternal life, and so on. It is clear there is a responsibility we are to fulfil.

To whom does Jesus give eternal life? To the man or woman, boy or girl who hears his words and believes in Him who sent him, to the one who is willing to listen to his claims, believe his credentials, and act on that basis, to follow him and be his obedient disciple. When one hears his words and obeys what he says, notice what happens: immediately Jesus says he has eternal life not, he shall have it someday when he dies. He has it, right then. Immediately also all judgment is past. Such a one has passed from death to life. Our Lord is making very clear to these Jews and to everyone else who reads his words the terms on which one passes from death to life. All of us are born headed for death. We do not like to talk about it, we put it away from our thoughts as long as possible, but we are all headed for death. Beyond death lies the second death unless we have eternal life. Thus the most important question anybody has to settle is whether he has believed in Jesus and received from his hand the gift of eternal life. In Verse 25 Jesus extends this well into the future:

Truly, truly, I say to you, the hour is coming, and now is, when the dead [the spiritually dead] will hear the voice of the Son of God, and those who hear will live. For as the Father has life in himself, so he has granted the Son also to have life in himself John 5:25-26

What does Jesus mean by the words, the hour is coming? This is a clear reference to the Day of Pentecost, to the new thing that would happen when the Spirit of God would come in a new, fresh way and this gift of eternal life would be given to Jews and Gentiles alike all over the world and through all the succeeding periods of time. Already the hour of which Jesus speaks is over 1900 years long. During that time whoever hears his word and believes on him who sent him receives eternal life.

But, Jesus also said, it now is, i.e., it was already happening. By those words he is referring to his own giving to individuals of the gift of life. We have already seen this in John's gospel. Nicodemus, the troubled religious leader, came by night to Jesus in an effort to find peace. Jesus said to him, Just as Moses lifted up the serpent in the wilderness, so must the Son of man be lifted up on a cross, that whoever believes in him may have eternal life, John 3:15 RSV. Nicodemus believed and received the gift of eternal life. The Samaritan woman at the well, who was living such an empty life, trying to find satisfaction in five husbands, hoping marriage would satisfy her yearnings, came empty, hungry, and thirsty to Jesus. To her he said, If you knew who is speaking to you, you would have asked of him and he would have given you a well of water springing up to eternal life, John 4:10 . Thus he gave her eternal life. She went away so excited she could not contain herself, but soon brought the whole town out to hear this One who could give the gift of eternal life.

So it was already happening, the hour is coming, and now is, when the spiritually dead will hear the voice of the Son of God and those who hear will live. Then he adds that as the Son of God, as the One who is eternally with the Father, he has always had this ability to give life to the spiritually dead. He has this life "in Himself." He is the One who has always given eternal life, in the Old Testament as well as the New. But now he adds something else. Verse 27:

And the Father

Has given him authority to execute judgment because he is the Son of man John 5:27

In other words, because he has now become a man and understands how we live, how we feel and what we face, he has the right to pass judgment on whether we should have the gift of life or remain in death. It is because Jesus came among us that he understands us. He knows the pressures and the problems we face; therefore he knows clearly when we have reached the place where we are ready to give up depending on ourselves and are able to receive the gift of life.

To receive the gift of life is the only way by which a man can be permanently changed, whether he has a black record or not. The only thing that can transform us right at the very heart of our being, and make us new again, is the gift of eternal life. Those who have it can never be the same again. The growth process can sometimes be very painful, as many of us know, but, when the gift of life is there at the heart of our being, we can never go back to what we once were. That life is in God's Son. But all physical life is also in his hands. Verse 28:

Do not marvel at this that tell you about what they were doing? They were agog with astonishment that he would speak like this. Their mouths dropped open at the daring claims he made. for the hour is coming when all who are in the tombs will hear his voice and come forth, those who have done good to the resurrection of life, and those who have done evil to the resurrection of judgment.

I can do nothing on my own authority; as I hear, I judge; and my judgment is just because I seek not my own will but the will of him who sent me, John 5:28-30

What a marvellous claim! Jesus says there is coming an hour in history when all the dead, all of them -- bad, good, evil, kind, loving, unloving, murderers, rapists -- all, shall come forth from the grave. He is going to empty the cemeteries of the world. Then, even the bodies of men and women will share in their final destiny.

Those who have done well shall experience the resurrection of life. What does done good mean? Many people extract this verse from the context and make up their own ideas about what it means to do well. They say if you have been fairly nice to your neighbour, do not beat your wife too often, speak kindly to people now and then, and try your best to obey the Ten Commandments, then perhaps the good you have done will outweigh the evil and God will let you into heaven.

But that is not what this verse is saying. This is just a few verses removed from what Jesus said about the gift of eternal life. To do well, of course, means to have received eternal life. Only those in whom the life of God is dwelling can do well in God's eyes. In the words of an old hymn, He died that we might be forgiven, He died to make us good; That we might go at last to heaven, Saved by His precious blood. Those who have obeyed his word walked in fellowship with him and shared his life to those are the ones who have done good.

What does done evil mean? Obviously this is referring to those who have refused his life, turned their backs on truth, and shut their ears to the offer of grace from God; those who have denied even the witness of nature, the witness of their own inner hearts. Those are the ones who have all their life done evil even though there were times when they thought they were doing well. They will come forth to the resurrection of judgment.

That is clearly the import of the words of Jesus. No wonder he frightened and challenged the people who heard him on that day, as he frightens and challenges us when we hear his words today. But note his assurance in Verse 30:

I can do nothing on my own authority; as I hear, I judge; and my judgment is just John 5:30a

There will be no argument against his judgment, no one can complain that it is unfair, because it is the work of both the Father and the Son; the Father who gave us life to begin with and who knows all that is in our hearts; the Son who came among us and knows how we feel and is both our Saviour and Judge. We decide which he is going to be by the reaction we have to truth. He's got the Whole World in His Hands He is our creator and ruler of all mankind.

Judgment of everyone is based on our Knowledge and on our Works

God judges all men on the basis of the truth they have received and their actions deeds in life. The works that count in the life as far as God is concerned are the acts of Christ in and through us the result of our faith.

Do you presume upon the riches of his kindness and forbearance and patience? Do you not know that God's kindness is meant to lead you to repentance? But by your hard and impenitent heart you are storing up wrath for yourself on the day of wrath when God's righteous judgment will be revealed. For he will render to every man according to his works: to those who by patience in well-doing seek for glory and honour and immortality, he will give eternal life; but for those who are factious and do not obey the truth, but obey wickedness, there will be wrath and fury. There will be tribulation and distress for every human being who does evil, the Jew first and also the Greek, but glory and honour and peace for everyone who does well, the Jew first and also the Greek. For God shows no partiality. All who have sinned without the law will also perish without the law, and all who have sinned under the law will be judged by the law. For it is not the hearers of the law who are righteous before God, but the doers of the law who will be justified. When Gentiles who have not the law do by nature what the law requires, they are a law to themselves, even though they do not have the law. They show that what the law requires is written on their hearts, while their conscience also bears witness and their conflicting thoughts accuse or perhaps excuse them on that day when, according to my gospel, God judges the secrets of men by Christ Jesus. Romans 2:4-16

In Chapter One of Romans we learn that the active, ever-present wrath of God "is [continuously] revealed from heaven against all ungodliness and unrighteousness of men who repress the truth in unrighteousness. Furthermore, all men everywhere know enough about God to be without excuse--one cannot plead ignorance on the Day of Judgment. He who believes in the Son has everlasting life; and he who does not believe the Son shall not see life, but the wrath of God abides on him. John 3:36

In Romans chapter Two we are introduced to the stored up aspect of the wrath of God. When the stored-up wrath is unleashed it cannot be stopped. For example, The iniquity of the house of Israel and Judah is exceedingly great, and the land is full of bloodshed, and the city full of perversity; for they say, The LORD has forsaken the land, and the LORD does not see! And as for me the Lord also, my eye will neither spare, nor will I have pity, but I will recompense their deeds on their own head. Ezekiel 9:9-10

Romans Chapter 2 tells us that when we judge and condemn others we are playing God. We have neither the knowledge nor the right to sit in judgment on others. Therefore our judgmental attitudes are serious sin. Judging others in order to make ourselves look good is not the same as discernment which we do need in order to help and encourage others.

Man looks upon the outward appearance, God looks upon the heart. At the judgment of the sheep and goats in Matthew 25:31ff men are evaluated, basically, on the basis of loving their neighbour in practical ways. The Sermon on the Mount intensifies the demands of the Law of Moses by showing that the motives of the heart are as important as outward conduct. James says whoever keeps the whole Law and fails in any one point, is guilty of all of it.

The standards of God are very high. All have sinned and fall short of the glory of God. One of the definitions of sin is compared to shooting an arrow at a target and missing the mark. Trying hard is not good enough. Who among us actually lives out the Golden Rule Mt. 7:12 in our daily lives? The gulf between a holy God and us sinners is an infinite chasm, bridgeable only by God Himself who, in Christ, has made our reconciliation possible.

What is the standard for acceptable human conduct? The standard is actually Jesus Himself. Jesus is God's righteousness. In contrast we are all like an unclean thing, and all our righteousness's are like filthy rags; we all fade as a leaf, our iniquities, like the wind, have taken us away from God. Isaiah 64:6

The three-fold work of the Holy Spirit in the world during the age we live in includes convicting the world of its unrighteousness:

Nevertheless I tell you the truth. It is to your advantage that I Jesus goes away; for if I do not go away, the Helper will not come to you; but if I depart, I will send Him to you. When He has come, He will convict the world of sin, and of righteousness, and of judgment: of sin, because they do not believe in me; of righteousness, because I go to My Father and you see me no more; of judgment, because the ruler of this world is judged.

People who live outwardly moral and decent lives are usually pursuing goals in life that run contrary to the will of God because they are most likely selfish and self-seeking. From whence comes the right to life, liberty, and the pursuit of happiness, or the freedom to have an abortion, or the right to choose one's sexual preferences? Man is a worshiping being by nature and if not serving the true and living God, is automatically serving idols.

Hypocrisy pretending to be godly when one is not is actually worse than open immorality.

These six things the LORD hates, yes, seven are an abomination to Him: A proud look, a lying tongue, Hands that shed innocent blood, a heart that devises wicked plans, Feet that are swift in running to evil, a false witness who speaks lies, and one who sows discord among brethren. Proverbs 6:16-19

Grace of God is kind to all men, He makes his rain fall on the just and the unjust." His kindness, patience and love to all mankind are for the purpose of bringing us to repentance. The proper response to God's grace is thanksgiving, worship, and commitment.

God's judgment is utterly fair and impartial. He judges us on our actual conduct based on what we do know about Him. God judges according to truth and He takes our motives into account. Doing well occasionally is not enough. A consistent good life marks the path of the righteous. The Lord prefers mercy to judgment: He is compassionate and longsuffering; He is, not willing that any should perish but that all should come to repentance. 2 Peter 3:9

3. Because judgment is often delayed in time God is longsuffering, many people assume God will never judge us.

4. Judgment is God's strange work however when God does move in judgment He is thorough and even ruthless.

5. More than one single judgment: Some popular schools of theology suppose that there is a coming single day of judgment for everyone. One finds this view reflected in religious literature and art. However, the Bible indicates that there are eight or more separate judgments of various groups of people recorded in his book;

A. When Jesus died on the cross the sins of all of mankind were judged. Jesus, the innocent Lamb of God, was the substitute who endured the full wrath and punishment of God for all of the sins of everyone who has ever lived. Rom. 3:21-26, 1 John 2:2 The judgment of all human sin by God through the propitiatory sacrifice of his Son on the cross has made it possible for all men everywhere to be freely forgiven and thus reconciled to God. For instance, Paul pleads with men to accept God good favour towards them now 2 Cor. 5:14-21. He who knew no sin was made to be sin for us, so that we might become the righteousness of God in Him. This does not mean that all men are saved, because God can not violate human freedom to refuse his grace.

B. The judgment of the Adamic nature of believers was carried by Christ on the cross. Rom. 6:1-10. This aspect of the work of Christ on the cross with us not merely for us is widely overlooked by Christians today!

C. Satan, the chief of the fallen angels, was judged at the cross. This is a vast subject contained within the short statement of God was in Christ reconciling the world unto Himself. Col. 1:19-20, John 12:31. For it pleased the Father that in Christ all the fullness should dwell, and by Him to reconcile all things to Himself, by Him, whether things on earth or things in heaven, having made peace through the blood of His cross. Col. 1:19-20

The Judgment Seat of Christ. This one judgment applies to Christians only. This judgment is not a judgment for the Christian's sin but of his works. John 3:18, 5:24, Rom. 8:1-4, 1 Cor. 3:9-15, 4:5; 2 Cor. 5:9-10, Rom. 14:7-12. It is a job performance evaluation.

The Judgment of Israel This event comes after the rapture of the church but before the judgment of the nations. Matt. 24:1-25:46. This is a vast subject! For starters see Daniel 12:1-3, Ezek. 20:33-44, Matt. 24:29-31, Zech. 12: 10-14, Joel 3, Malachi 3:1-6, Ezek. 36-37, Isa. 63-66, Hosea 5:13-6:3, Rom. 11:25-36, Rev. 14:14-20, Matt. 25:31-46). Jesus is the Avenger of Blood and Kinsman Redeemer, especially for Israel. Jesus has a special and unique relationship with His own people Israel, and they are a special nation as God's model nation. They are to be judged more strictly than the gentile nations for these two reasons.

The Judgment of Angels: Christians, working together with their Lord Jesus will judge both angels and the world. 1 Cor. 6:2,3 as said in the Bible.

The Final Judgment of the Nations: The gentile nations will be judged immediately following the judgment of the nation Israel, just after the Lord Jesus has returned to the Mount of Olives at the Second Advent. The basis for this judgment is how the nations have treated the Jews! Joel 3:1-8, Matt. 25:31-46

The Last Judgment. Rev. 20:11-15 All the unbelievers of all time, will be judged by the deeds and banished forever from the presence of God. There are degrees of punishment for the wicked. This judgment comes in earth-history time at the end of the Millennium, but before the New Heavens and New Earth.

Temporal Judgments

God also judges nations down through history. Nations ruse and nations fall. This is discussed in Ray Stedman's studies of the parables of Matthew 13, Behind the Scenes of History, and can be seen in his book Death of a Nation on the book of Jeremiah; Points in time when God judges an individual or a nation are illustrative of greater judgments which will come later in time. The destruction of Sodom and Gomorrah and the cities of the Plain is an example of a temporal, point-in-time judgment. Jude says, And the angels who did not keep their proper domain, but left their own abode, He has reserved in everlasting chains under darkness for the judgment of the great day; as Sodom and Gomorrah, and the cities around them in a similar manner to these, having given themselves over to sexual immorality and gone after strange flesh, are set forth as an example, suffering the vengeance of eternal fire. Jude 6,7 The latter event was a judgment by God at a certain point in time past, about 2000 BC, Genesis 18-19.

The judgment of the Canaanites whom God ordered Joshua and the incoming Israelites to "utterly destroy" is often criticized by non-Christians as an indication that Yahweh is cruel and arbitrary. Glenn Miller discusses this judgment in an article, how could a God of Love order the massacre Individuals are also judged when any group of people is being judged.

Individuals are also judged during their life-times. A particular sin which leads to death means that a certain believer may not be allowed to live out his full life span on earth but may be called home early because of disobedience. Wars are temporal judgments from God applicable to both parties. That is, there are no just wars. God's role in these judgments usually escapes the notice of the world, but discerning believers will see God's hand in world affairs. Acts of God in legalese are accidents, such as shipwrecks in a storm, where there is no obvious human cause. Since there are in reality no accidents in a universe where God is in full control of all the details, God allows and even causes shipwrecks, and such, but we don't always know why. When a natural disaster occurs many prognosticators rush to explain why the victims in the disaster suffered and died. In most cases we cannot track down the chain of causality and we ought not to try. Romans 11:33 reminds us How unsearchable are His judgments and His ways past finding out is a clear statement

Avoiding Judgment

We can avoid being judged by God and we can avoid being disqualified for the Lord's work if we judge ourselves regularly. The Apostle Paul suggests he was all too aware of the possibility he might fail to finish the task he was called to--that he might be disqualified. He says, "But I discipline my body and bring it into subjection, lest, when I have preached to others, I myself should become disqualified.1 Cor. 9:27 He also says, for if we would judge ourselves, we would not be judged.1 Cor. 11:31 and further adds that every follower of Christ can expect corrective discipline from God. But when we are judged, we are chastened by the Lord, that we may not be condemned with the world.1 Cor. 11:32 the discipline of God for the believer is not punitive but corrective. This is discussed in Hebrews 12:1-17.

OF EIGHT JUDGMENTS announced in the Bible, one is wholly past, two pertain to the present, and five are wholly future. The five, being future, are themes of unfulfilled prophecy. To the end that the entire field of judgment may be appraised under this general division, those judgments which are not predictive in character will be included in this thesis; and the two pertaining to the present, because of their interrelationship, will be considered together. By their recognizance of but one so-called final judgment, theologians in general have laid themselves open to the suspicion that they have not been worthy first-hand students of the Sacred Text. It is here contended that there are various judgments which are widely separated with respect to time, theme, subjects, and circumstances. This body of truth bearing on these judgments is not only comprehensive but free from complications. These judgments are:

I. JUDGMENTS THROUGH THE CROSS: Three features of divine judgment, already indicated under salvation, were achieved by Christ's death on the cross. These are 1) the judgment of the sin of the world, (2) the judgment of the believer's sin nature, and (3) the judgment of Satan. These, it will be seen, were perfectly met by Christ when He died.

1. THE JUDGMENT OF THE SIN OF THE WORLD: Regardless of objections raised by some theologians who have a theory to defend, the New Testament asserts with unqualified assurance that Christ died for the sin of the world John 1:29; 3:16; Heb. 2:9; I John 2:2. It is true that out of all at least fourteen objectives in His death Christ had a specific design regarding the sins of the elect, or those who would believe John 11:11; Eph. 5:25-27; I John 2:2; but His inclusion of the sins of the elect as a particular class does not exclude the essential truth that He also had a world-wide purpose in His death. Though it may not be comprehended wholly by finite minds, the message is to be received, as declared in the Word of God, which asserts that full pardon and deliverance from the penalty of sin has been perfectly secured for all those who believe. Without discussing again the theological implications of this declaration, it may be pointed out that this is a divine judgment for sin which falls upon another, who bears it as a Substitute. In this judgment

unrestricted demands are imposed and these are endured to infinite completeness.

2. **THE JUDGMENT OF THE BELIEVER'S SIN NATURE:** Evidence that this important judgment is not extended to the unregenerate is conclusive, since no Scripture relates it to them. The value to the believer of the accomplishment of a sufficient and final divine judgment of the sin nature Rom. 6:1-10 is far more reaching. That value does not accomplish any change in the present vital forcefulness of that nature. This judgment consists rather in a divine reckoning which disposes of every moral objection that the sin nature would otherwise impose upon the indwelling Holy Spirit so as to preclude His control of that nature. Thus the entire possibility of the overcoming power of the Spirit in the daily life of the Christian is involve Since there is no divine intention that the unsaved shall be empowered to holy living in their unsaved state having not the Spirit. Jude 1:19 there is neither provision nor promise which extends the value of this judgment beyond the limits of those who are saved. It could not be questioned that Christ's death for the believer's sin nature is a form of divine judgment. Rom. 6:1-10; Gal. 5: 24; Eph. 4:22-24; Col. 3:9-10.

3. **THE JUDGMENT OF SATAN THROUGH THE CROSS:** Since it is but partially revealed, to human minds the relationship between God and the angels is incomprehensible. The particular relation between Christ and Satan is equally veiled. Though vast in its scope, some light is gained on the relations existing between Christ and the angels of darkness in Genesis 3:15, the temptation in the wilderness Luke 4: 1-13, the war in heaven Rev. 12: 7-12, the thousand-year reign in which angelic powers are subdued I Cor. 15:25-26, but more especially from the judgment of Satan by Christ in connection with the cross John 12:31; 14:30; 16:11; Col. 2:14-15. Thus it is disclosed that the cross of Christ in its threefold outreach is one of the greatest, if not the greatest, of all divine judgments.

II. THE SELF-JUDGMENT OF THE BELIEVER AND THE CHASTENING JUDGMENTS OF GOD:

Two distinct judgments are in view under this general head and, as before stated, because of their interdependence. The child in the Father's household and family must understand that God is a perfect disciplinarian. Disobedience must in His own time and way result in chastisement. The central passage on the Father's discipline is Hebrews 12:3-15. In this context it is declared that every son in the Father's household is subject to chastisement as occasion may arise. Verse 6 makes reference to both chastisement and scourging. These are to be distinguished. Scourging aims at a once-for-all conquering of the human will, and when the will is yielded there is no more need for scourging. On the other hand, chastisement may be many times repeated and may be administered to the end that the believer may be strengthened thereby, or to prevent him from going into evil paths. A good man may by discipline become a better man. Christ said, every branch that does not bears fruit, he will purge it, that it may bring forth more fruit. John 15:2. As for chastisement which is a correction for wrong, it is written of those who partake of the communion unworthily, For this cause many are weak and sickly among you, and many have fall asleep. I Cor. II: 30. Immediately following this declaration and closely related to it is the added truth that the Christian may avoid chastisement for wrongdoing by making a confession of it to God, which confession is self-judgment. Should the confession be withheld, there must be chastisement. The passage we just reads, says for if we would judge ourselves, we should not be judged. But when we are judged, we are chastened of the Lord, that we should not be condemned with the world I Cor. 11:31-32. It is in this passage that two aspects of judgment appear with the one dependent upon the other. First, the believer is to confess to God every known sin, and, second, the Father may judge His child by chastisement him or she when the confession is refused. John I: 9. the divine provision is gracious to the last degree. When the Christian has sinned, God awaits the confession of that sin. Should the confession be withheld, for God, in His own time and way, before judgement is pronounce on an individual?

In Daniel chapter 9, verses 24-27, God gave the world two prophetic timetables; a 69-week timetable leading up to Jesus Christ's first coming, and a remaining 70th week leading up to His second coming. Hence, this prophecy is widely known as the 70-Weeks prophecy. These four verses, 24-27, were spoken directly to the prophet Daniel:

Seventy weeks are determined upon thy people the Jews and upon thy holy city Jerusalem, to finish the transgression, to make an end of sins, to make reconciliation for iniquity, to bring in everlasting righteousness, to seal up the vision and prophecy and to anoint the most holy.

Know therefore and understand, that from the going forth of the commandment to restore and to build Jerusalem unto the Messiah the Prince shall be seven weeks, and threescore and two 62 weeks: the street shall be built again, and the wall, even in troubles times.

And after threescore and two 62 weeks shall Messiah be cut of killed, but not for Himself. And the people of the prince that shall come shall destroy the city and the sanctuary. And the end thereof shall be with a flood, and unto the end of the war desolations are determined.

And He shall confirm the covenant with many for one week. And in the midst of the week He shall cause the sacrifice and the oblation to cease. And for the overspreading of abominations He shall make it desolate, even until the consummation. And that determined shall be poured upon the desolate. Daniel 9:24-27 I have already explained the first three verses of this prophecy. I have explained how those three verses have already been fulfilled by the first coming of Christ, His death upon the cross, and the subsequent destruction of the city Jerusalem and its sanctuary the Temple by the Romans in 70 AD. The first 69 weeks were 'weeks of years', each week lasting 7 years, each 'prophetic year' consisting of 360 days, for a total of 173,880 days (69 x 7 x 360). This represented the period extending from the Persian authorization for the Jews to rebuild Jerusalem in 445 BC, until Palm Sunday in 32 AD, when Jesus entered Jerusalem just prior to His death.

In this web page I explain the fourth and final verse of this prophecy. An explanation of this verse must answer the following four questions:

1) Who is this 'He' who confirms a covenant, and causes sacrifices to cease?
2) What is this covenant that 'He' confirms?
3) What is the nature of this 'week' during which the covenant is confirmed?
4) What are these abominations that lead to desolation (the 'abomination of desolation')?

My answers to these questions are as follows:

1) The 'He' who confirms a covenant and brings an end to sacrifices is the resurrected Son of God, Jesus Christ, now seated at the right hand of the Father and empowered to do these things. Because He established the New Covenant through His death, it was necessary that He bring the sacrifices of the old Mosaic Covenant to an end.
2) The covenant that Jesus confirmed is the Abrahamic Covenant. He confirmed it backward in time for all those who looked ahead to its fulfillment, and He confirmed it forward in time for all those who would look back to its fulfilment at the cross.
3) The 70th Week in this prophecy is not like the first 69 weeks; it is not a week of seven years. Rather, it is the Great Week of the Abrahamic Covenant; extending backward in time to God's original covenant promises to Abraham, divided in the very middle by the Roman destruction of Jerusalem in 70 AD, and extending forward to the second coming of Jesus Christ, when He will come to establish the kingdom of David in Israel and the kingdom of God on earth.

4) The abomination that brings desolation, as the Lord Jesus explained on the Mount of Olives shortly before His death, is the invasion of Jerusalem by the armies of Rome in 70 AD.

The Great Week of the Abrahamic Covenant

It will not be possible for my visitor to understand the points that I make in this book without some prior knowledge of the Abrahamic Covenant. I have explain the importance of that covenant, as well as the reasoning behind the dates that I have assigned to it 1910 BC and to the second coming of Christ 2050 AD in my Introduction to Bible Prophecy. These dates are not meant to be precise. They are estimations meant to convey a greater truth.

In addition it is important to understand Jesus' fulfilment of the first 69-week timetable in the 70-Weeks prophecy, and His revelation that the 'abomination of desolation' which marks the midpoint of the 70th week would be the approaching destruction of Jerusalem by Rome in 70 AD. I have provided this information as The Olivet Discourse. I would encourage my visitor to examine both of these pages before coming to this one.

Once my visitor has a grasp of the Abrahamic Covenant, Jesus' fulfilment of the 69-week timetable, and His identification of the abomination of desolation spoken of by Daniel as the Roman invasion of Jerusalem in 70 AD, it should be relatively easy to examine a passage of scriptures that has been greatly misunderstood and neglected, and yet is the key to understanding the 70th Week in

Daniel: John's vision in Revelation 10, and then he opens it up for us to see in Revelation chapters 11-13. John's Little Book provides us with four separate visions of Daniel's 70th Week, each one described in terms of its two separate halves. These four visions are...

1. The Temple & Court Revelation 11:1-2
2. The Two Witnesses Revelation 11:3-14
3. The Woman, the Child and the Dragon Revelation 12
4. The Beast from the Sea Revelation 13:1-10

Jesus taught His disciples that no one would know the day or the hour of His second coming; only God the Father Matthew 24:36. Given the specific years that I use in the graphic above 1910BC, 70AD, 2050AD, you might think that I am trying to set dates. I am not. My dates are based upon an arbitrary date that I have chosen for Solomon's construction of the first Temple in Jerusalem; the year 1000BC. I chose that year because it is a nice round number, and makes it easy for me to date other Biblical events in a timeline that people can easily understand and remember. But my dates are not meant to be precise. That's not to say that Jesus couldn't come back in 2050. I believe that such a date is well within reason.

In this book I am trying to communicate a framework and an idea. It is the bigger concept that must be grasped; of a great Week divided in the middle. Within that context, if Solomon built the Temple in 980 BC instead of 1000 BC, then that would shorten the first half of the Week by 20 years, and thus would have to shorten the second half by 20 years also; making the projected date of Christ's return 2030 AD, instead of 2050.

People will invariably take information from this book and attempt to establish a precise date for Christ's return. I cannot prevent that. I thank God that a proper understanding of the 70th Week gives us such a clear and satisfying sense of when Jesus will return, that the desire to set dates disappears. We must obey what the Lord Jesus taught; that attempting to set dates will be futile. What matters is that we live our lives watchfully and prayerfully, always ready to stand before Him and be judged:

Watch therefore, and pray always, that you may be accounted worthy to escape all these things that shall come to pass, and to stand before the Son of Man.

Luke 21:36

RECEIVING THE BOOK

Revelation 10 describes the Apostle John's reception of a 'Little Book'. He was told to eat it. It was sweet in his mouth, but bitter in his stomach. Then John was told that he must prophecy 'again'; in other words, give an additional prophecy, above and beyond what he had already received. The 'Little Book' contained that additional prophecy, and its contents are revealed to us in Revelation 11-13.

John's Little Book sits in the larger book of Revelation, much like the little advertising or other 'special inserts' that we find in magazines like Time or National Geographic. It is held in place, and connected to the rest of Revelation, by the 'staple' of the 7th Trumpet Revelation 11:15-19. John's Little Book provides us with 4 visions of Daniel's 70th week. Each vision describes that Week in terms of one or both of its halves.

MEASURING THE TEMPLE

In this vision John is told to measure the Temple and the Jewish people who worship there, but to leave out the court the Temple Mount, because it will be given to the Gentiles for 42 months 42 months is 1/2 of 7 years.

And there was given me a reed likes unto a rod: and the angel stood, saying Rise, and measure the Temple of God, and the altar, and them that worship therein. But the court which is outside the Temple leave out, and measure it not; for it is given unto the Gentiles: and the holy city shall they tread under foot forty and two months Revelation 11:1-2

These two witnesses perform the same miracles that Moses and Elijah performed, but they are not Moses and Elijah. These witnesses symbolize the name that the Jewish people gave to the Bible; The Law and the Prophets. This is a vision of God giving the Bible both the Old and New Testaments to the world; an activity which was authenticated by God through supernatural power and divine miracles performed by prophets and apostles alike. It ended just before the destruction of Jerusalem in 70 AD.

And I will give power unto my two witnesses, and they shall prophesy a thousand two hundred and sixty days, clothed in sackcloth. These are the two olive trees, and the two candlesticks standing before the God of the earth. And if any man will hurt them, fire proceeds out of their mouth, and devours their enemies: and if any man will hurt them, he must in this manner be killed. These have power to shut heaven that it rain not in the days of their prophecy: and have power over waters to turn them to blood, and to smite the earth with all plagues, as often as they will. And when they shall have finished their testimony, the beast that ascends out of the bottomless pit shall make war against them, and shall overcome them, and kill them. And their dead bodies shall lie in the street of the great city, which spiritually is called Sodom and Egypt, where also our Lord was crucified Jerusalem.

And they of the people and kindreds and tongues and nations shall see their dead bodies three days and an half, and shall not suffer their dead bodies to be put in graves. And they that dwell upon the earth shall rejoice over them, and make merry, and shall send gifts one to another; because these two prophets tormented them that dwelt on the earth. And after three days and an half the Spirit of life from God entered into them, and they stood upon their feet; and great fear fell upon them which saw them. And they heard a great voice from heaven saying unto them "Come up here". And they ascended up to heaven in a cloud; and their enemies beheld them. And the same hour was there a great earthquake, and the tenth part of the city fell, and in the earthquake were slain of men seven thousand: and the remnant were frightened, and gave glory to the God of heaven.

Revelation 11:3-14

Vision 2

THE TWO WITNESSES TESTIFY

It is appropriate to represent the New Testament as a part of 'the Law and the Prophets'. This continuity was evident in the words and life of Christ. In His Sermon on the Mount, Jesus explained His relationship to 'the Law and the Prophets'. He said that His work was a continuation and fulfillment of them:

Think not that I am come to destroy the law, or the prophets: I am not come to destroy, but to fulfill.

Matthew 5:17

In the transfiguration on the mount, Jesus appeared to His disciples with Moses and Elijah, as God the Father spoke from heaven:

Then answered Peter and said unto Jesus "Lord, it is good for us to be here: if You will, let us make here three tabernacles; one for You, and one for Moses, and one for Elijah". While he yet spoke, behold, a bright cloud overshadowed them: and behold a voice out of the cloud, which said "This is my beloved Son, in whom I am well pleased; hear Him".

Matthew 17:4-5

Here the Lord Jesus was not only associated with 'the Law and the Prophets', but given preeminence over them, since Moses and Elijah were servants of God, while Jesus was identified by the Father as His Son (Hebrews 3:1-6).

In the second half of this vision, the witnesses lie dead in the streets of Jerusalem. This symbolizes the fact that God has held Jerusalem responsible for their deaths. It represents the fulfillment of the words of the Lord Jesus, when He warned the Jewish leaders that He would be sending more messengers to them (the apostles and disciples), and that their mistreatment of these Christian witnesses would result in terrible judgment upon Israel:

Therefore, behold, I send unto you prophets, and wise men, and scribes: and some of them you shall kill and crucify; and some of them shall you scourge in your synagogues, and persecute them from city to city; that upon you may come all the righteous blood shed upon the earth, from the blood of righteous Abel unto the blood of Zacharias son of Barachias, whom you slew between the Temple and the altar.

Matthew 23:34-35 (also see the apostle Paul's words in 1 Thessalonians 2:14-16)

There should be no doubt that the many sufferings of the Jewish people, from 70 AD up to the present time, represent the fulfillment of Jesus' words. Again we are talking about a period of time much longer than half of 7 years. In this vision God describes the first half of the 70th week as a period of 1260 days (3.5 years), while twice He describes the second half as lasting 3.5 days. Here God is clearly indicating that the 70th Week is not to be understood as seven literal years.

THE SEVENTH TRUMPET

This trumpet is a continuation of the trumpets of Revelation chapters 8 and 9. John's Little Book sits inside the larger book of Revelation, much like the 'inserts' that are often found in the center of today's magazines. These often contain a special informational or advertising supplement that is added to the magazine, and can be removed and read separately. The 7th Trumpet is the 'staple' that attaches John's Little Book to the rest of the book of Revelation.

And the seventh angel sounded, and there were great voices in heaven, saying "The kingdoms of this world are become the kingdoms of our Lord, and of his Christ; and He shall reign for ever and ever. And the four and twenty elders, which sat before God on their seats, fell upon their faces, and worshipped God, saying "We give You thanks, O Lord God Almighty, which are, and were, and are to come; because You have taken your great power and have reigned. And the nations were angry, and Your wrath is come, and the time of the dead, that they should be judged, and that You should give reward unto Your servants the prophets, and to the saints, and them that fear Your name, small and great; and should destroy them which destroy the earth. And the Temple of God was opened in heaven, and there was seen in His temple the ark of His testament: and there were lightnings, and voices, and thunderings, and an earthquake, and great hail.

Revelation 11:15-19

The 7th Trumpet's placement here (at the resurrection of the Two Witnesses) is appropriate, because it dovetails perfectly with the promised bodily resurrection of all of God's 'faithful witnesses' at the sounding of the last Trumpet, as foretold by Paul (1 Corinthians 15:52, 1 Thessalonians 4:16).

THE WOMAN, THE CHILD, AND THE DRAGON

The woman in this vision is the nation of Israel, struggling down through the centuries to successfully bring Abraham's promised Seed into the world. The Child is born and Satan tries to devour Him. This may represent Herod's attempt to kill the Christ-child at His birth, or it may represent Satan's frequent temptations of the Lord Jesus, to keep Him from succeeding in His work of salvation. The flight of the woman into the wilderness represents the dispersion of the Jewish people throughout the world, beginning with the fall of Jerusalem in 70 AD.

And there appeared a great wonder in heaven; a woman clothed with the sun, and the moon under her feet, and upon her head a crown of twelve stars. And she is with child cried out, travailing in birth and pained to be delivered. And there appeared another wonder in heaven: Behold, a great red dragon having seven heads and ten horns, and seven crowns upon his heads. And his tail drew the third part of the stars of heaven, and did cast them to the earth. And the dragon stood before the woman who was ready to deliver, to devour her child as soon as it was born. And she brought forth a man child, who was to rule all nations with a rod of iron; and her child was caught up unto God, and to His throne. And the woman fled into the wilderness, where she has a place prepared by God, that they should feed her there a thousand two hundred and sixty days.

Revelation 12:1-6

Vision 3

THE WOMAN PRESERVED IN THE WILDERNESS

Not only is the destruction of Jerusalem a judgment from God upon Israel; it is, at the same time, the means of Israel's deliverance. This vision tells us that, if the Jewish people had not been dispersed throughout the world for the second half of the 70th Week (1260 days), they might not have survived as a nation.

The sun, moon and 12 stars are a reminder to us of Joseph's dream (Genesis 37:9-10). Joseph is symbolic of the Lord Jesus. Both men were betrayed into the hands of the Gentiles by their Jewish brothers. Both men were thought by their brothers to be dead. Jesus is now working behind the scenes, as Joseph did, to bring His brethren to repentance. Someday this greater 'Joseph' is going to reveal Himself to His people in a tearful reunion that will save their nation and bring them into everlasting blessing (Zechariah 12:6-13:1).

As I see it, this vision presents a problem for the Dispensationalists. How do they incorporate Israel's giving birth to the Messiah, and His subsequent resurrection, into their future 70th Week? The woman flees into the wilderness after her child's resurrection, and is fed there for one half of the 70th week (1260 days). Which half of their 70th Week is this?

WAR IN HEAVEN

This passage presents to us one of the most powerful lessons in all of the Bible. First of all it explains Satan's work as mankind's accuser. Until Jesus had accomplished our salvation on the cross, Satan had always been able to come to the Father and point out how undeserving we are of His mercy. I believe that, as Jesus hung upon the cross being tormented by His enemies, Satan was shouting in the Father's ear, asking 'How could you let your Son die for such wicked people as these?'. His accusations were valid and had merit. But once the Father forsook His Son, abandoning Him to death, our salvation was accomplished and mercy triumphed over judgment. Satan had no more business before the throne of God.

And there was war in heaven: Michael and his angels fought against the dragon; and the dragon and his angels fought, and prevailed not; neither was their place found any more in heaven. And the great dragon was cast out, that old serpent, called the Devil, and Satan, which deceives the whole world: he was cast out into the earth, and his angels were cast out with him. And I heard a loud voice saying in heaven "Now is come salvation, and strength, and the kingdom of our God, and the power of his Christ: for the accuser of our brethren is cast down, which accused them before our God day and night. And they overcame him by the blood of the Lamb, and by the word of their testimony; and they loved not their lives unto the death. Therefore rejoice, you heavens, and you that dwell in them. Woe to the inhabitants of the earth and of the sea! For the devil is come down unto you, having great wrath, because he knows that he has but a short time".

Revelation 12:7-12

The judgment and 'casting out' of Satan is central to the Christian message. Jesus twice referred to it in the gospel of John. God wants all people, Christian and non-Christian alike, to understand what happened to Satan just prior to 70 AD, and the implication of these things for us down here on earth.

Now is the judgment of this world: now shall the prince of this world be cast out (of heaven).

John 12:31

And when the Holy Spirit is come, He will reprove the world of sin, and of righteousness, and of judgment. Of sin, because they believe not on Me. Of righteousness, because I go to My Father, and you see Me no more. Of judgment, because the prince of this world is judged.

John 16:8-11

THE GREAT TRIBULATION

Satan has now been cast down to earth, a tremendously angry, bitter and frustrated Archangel. He is like Pharaoh in the book of Exodus. Though he was defeated, Pharaoh chose to pursue Israel into the Red Sea, rather than acknowledge his defeat and let his captives go. Satan also knows that He has lost, but that will not stop him from hardening his heart and deceiving mankind until the very end; plunging headlong into The Lake of Fire. Soon that Lake will close over him, as the Red Sea closed over Pharaoh.

Next God explains the persecution of the Jewish people, since the first 'flood' of destruction hit Jerusalem. Satan has been pouring out his fury upon the people who brought his nemesis, the 'Seed of Abraham', into the world.

And when the dragon saw that he was cast unto the earth, he persecuted the woman which brought forth the man child. And to the woman were given two wings of a great eagle, that she might fly into the wilderness, into her place, where she is nourished for a time, and times, and half a time, from the face of the serpent. And the serpent cast out of his mouth water as a flood after the woman, that he might cause her to be carried away of the flood. And the earth helped the woman, and the earth opened her mouth, and swallowed up the flood which the dragon cast out of his mouth. And the dragon was angry with the woman, and went to make war with the remnant of her seed,

Repeated waves of persecution have pursued the Jews since 70 AD, but the Jewish 'Diaspora' throughout the earth has caused these floods to fall short of their ultimate aim. Once again we see that God's scattering of the Jewish people has been an act of mercy, preserving them down through the centuries. Now we can understand the spiritual reality behind the scenes of history, and who it was working within men like Hitler to seek the destruction of the Jewish race. Satan is still at work today, seeking to rally mankind against Israel and the Jewish people. These verses also tell us that faithful Christians will be found suffering along with the Jews, rather than persecuting them.

This passage describes the second half of the 70th Week in very grim terms. It is the time of Satan's wrath, and is the 'Great Tribulation' spoken of in Revelation 7:14. It is the second half of Daniel's 70th Week, stretching from the destruction of Jerusalem to the second coming of Christ.

I believe that the 6th Seal represents the Day of the Lord, the onset of nuclear war, and the point in time when God will remove His people from the planet, while He simultaneously 'seals' a portion of the Jewish people for preservation during the events that follow. At that point God will take this wave of destruction, that Satan and mankind have set in motion, and use it to punish a wicked human race. When God says 'Woe to the inhabitants of the earth and the sea' (Rev. 12:17), He is referring to a Satanic rage that first expressed itself against Jews and Christians beginning in 70 AD, but will culminate in the destruction of the planet as foretold by Isaiah:

They that see you (Lucifer) shall narrowly look upon you and consider you, saying "Is this the man that made the earth to tremble that did shake kingdoms? That made the world as a wilderness and destroyed the cities thereof? That opened not the house of his prisoners?"

Isaiah 14:16-17

For those of us living comfortably in America, the idea that we are now in the Great Tribulation seems inappropriate. But it is not a strange concept for much of the rest of the world. Americans life in relative luxury, ease and wealth.

Earlier in this vision, the woman was fed in the wilderness for 1260 days. Now, as God describes the same events, she is nourished in the wilderness for 3.5 times. Again, God is showing us that the 70th Week is not a period of 7 literal years.

THE BEAST FROM THE SEA

In Revelation 13 the first of two Beasts is revealed to us:

And I stood upon the sand of the sea, and saw a beast rise up out of the sea, having seven heads and ten horns, and upon his horns ten crowns, and upon his heads the name of blasphemy. And the beast which I saw was like unto a leopard, and his feet were as the feet of a bear, and his mouth as the mouth of a lion: and the dragon gave him his power, and his seat, and great authority. And I saw one of his heads as it were wounded to death; and his deadly wound was healed: and all the world wondered after the beast. And they worshipped the dragon which gave power unto the beast: and they worshipped the beast, saying "Who is like unto the beast? who is able to make war with him?" And there was given unto him a mouth speaking great things and blasphemies; and power was given unto him to continue forty and two months.

Revelation 13:1-5

A primary message of the book of Hebrews chapters 7-10 is that the Old Testament Leviticus priesthood, characterized by 1. Dying men who were 2. Morally imperfect, offering 3. Useless repetitive sacrifices their uselessness being demonstrated by the fact that they had to be repeated) has been replaced by the new priesthood of Christ. Jesus is morally perfect, will never die again, and has sacrificed Himself once, effective for all eternity. Jesus says to the world 'Come to Me and be saved', while Rome's priests say 'Come to Rome and be saved'. Even though the Bible clearly says that the old Leviticus style of priesthood is obsolete, and explains why this is so, contrasting it with the glorious priesthood of Jesus Christ, Rome has chosen to copy the old priesthood of Israel anyway, steering humanity toward its own morally imperfect, dying priests, who offer repetitive sacrifices, rather than to a direct and personal relationship with Christ.

In Revelation 17:4, the Roman Catholic Mass is symbolized by a golden cup in the hand of the Woman, which God says is 'full of abominations and the filthiness of her fornication'. Unlike genuine biblical communion, the Roman Catholic Mass is not merely symbolic. Rome claims that its priests have divine authority and power to change transubstantiate the bread and wine into the very body and blood of Christ, which they then re-sacrifice and re-offer to God for the forgiveness of sins and the salvation of men. Rome pronounces a curse upon anyone who denies this, and encourages its members to worship the bread and wine that has supposedly been 'transubstantiated' into Christ Himself that is Rome in Prophecy.

It has been the protests hence the term protestant of faithful Christians against this Satanic, soul-destroying lie of Rome that have defined genuine Protestantism from the beginning. This is not a situation where Christians can 'live and let live'. Those who have experienced this rich, deep, life-changing personal relationship with Christ are obligated by God to proclaim the difference between a true relationship with Him, and Rome's false one. There is no middle ground, and there can be no compromise. If we love God and our fellow man, we must proclaim the true way of salvation.

This is why countless faithful Christians have been put to death by Rome for centuries; because they have known their Bibles, and have shared its truth with others. This is why the Protestant reformation thrived; because it began with the placing of Bibles into the hands of everyday people, allowing them to compare Rome's claims with the word of God itself. This is how people come to a personal relationship with Christ; by letting God speak directly to them through His word, and then by responding directly to Him in prayer. This is why Rome has uniformly opposed the placing of Bibles in the hands of lay people; because it has enabled them to bypass Rome and go directly to God. God has warned that He will visit terrible judgment upon Rome for its wickedness in the end (Revelation 14:8, 16:19, 17:16-17, chapter 18.

Paul spoke of the 'man of sin' having miraculous demonic power. I think this characterizes Rome also. I believe that Constantine and his soldiers probably did see a miraculous sign in the sky, instructing them to wage war under the banner of the cross. The question is 'Was it a sign from God, or from Satan?' Rome's nuns and priests have dabbled in the occult throughout history, using 'eastern' meditative techniques to contact the spirit world; a practice that has never been more prevalent in the Roman Catholic Church than it is today. It wouldn't surprise me to see supernatural power manifested by the Roman Catholic Church on an unprecedented scale in the days ahead.

5) THE ANTICHRIST

The Antichrist is mentioned in only four verses, all written by the apostle John, and found only in his letters. The word 'antichrist' never appears anywhere else in the scriptures. It means what it appears to mean; one who is against or opposed to Christ.

Little children, it is the last hour; and as you have heard that the Antichrist is coming, even now many antichrists have come, by which we know that it is the last hour. They went out from us, but they were not of us; for if they had been of us, they would have continued with us. But they went out that they might be made manifest, that none of them were of us.

1 John 2:18-19

Who is a liar but he who denies that Jesus is the Christ? He is antichrist who denies the Father and the Son.

1 John 2:22

And every spirit that does not confess that Jesus Christ has come in the flesh is not of God. And this is the spirit of the Antichrist, which you have heard was coming, and is now already in the world.

1 John 4:3

For many deceivers have gone out into the world who do not confess Jesus Christ as coming in the flesh. This is a deceiver and an antichrist.

2 John 8

As we examine John's words, the one thing that defines the antichrist is false doctrine. More specifically, John defines antichrists as

- A. Those who once professed faith in Christ, but have departed from biblical Christianity.
- B. Those who deny the Father and the Son.
- C. Those who deny that the Son of God has come into the world in human flesh.

John's description of an antichrist could apply to any one of a number of people, religions or cults that have claimed to be Christian or to respect Christ, but have departed from the true Christian faith.

It should be observed that John never says anything about the Antichrist establishing covenants, ending sacrifices, claiming to be God, having miraculous powers, cooperating with the Beast or being destroyed at the second coming of Christ. Nor does he link 'the Antichrist' with any other passage of scripture. The term 'antichrist' is not even found in that greatest of all prophetic books, Revelation, which John himself wrote.

Rather than take caution from this, Dispensationalists have taken advantage of it. Because of his sinister name, and because so little is known about him, Dispensationalists have felt free to plug the Antichrist into their end-times scenario. For them the Antichrist is 'the Prince who is to come' (of Daniel 9:26), the 'Abomination of Desolation', Paul's 'man of sin', and 'the Beast' that gets thrown into the Lake of Fire (along with the False Prophet). One cannot count all of the books, articles and movies that have flowed out of John's very limited words about 'the Antichrist', Tim Lahaye's 'Left Behind' series being only one of many.

Although John says that there are many antichrists, in 1 John 2:18 he seems to refer to one specific person, 'the Antichrist', who surpasses all other antichrists in his opposition to God. So who is this Antichrist? I do not know. One candidate to consider would be Mohammed. Islam claims Biblical roots, but fiercely denies that God has a Son, and that Christ was 'Emmanuel'; 'God with us' in a human body. There is no other religion that more directly and forcefully denies the deity of Christ today than Islam. Muslims have written 'God has no son' inside their mosque, the 'Dome of the Rock', sitting on the Temple Mount in Jerusalem. This will ultimately prove to be a profound embarrassment to them. It was this One who declared Himself to be the Son of God, and who predicted the desolation of the Temple and its possession by the Gentiles until His second coming, whose words they now fulfill with their mosque on the Temple Mount.

6) THE ABOMINATION OF DESOLATION (Daniel 9:27, Matthew 24:15, Mark 13:14) The Roman general Titus and his army, which destroyed Jerusalem and the Temple in 70 AD (see The Timetable for Jesus' Return for a discussion of Titus).
7. THE 'PRINCE WHO IS TO COME' OF DANIEL 9:26 - also the Roman general Titus.
8. THE LITTLE HORN OF DANIEL 7:8 The United States of America sees The United States in Bible Prophecy
9. THE LITTLE HORN OF DANIEL 8:9 The City of Rome, beginning as a very small power on the edge of the Greek Empire. Rome first expelled Greece from the Italian peninsula in the Pyrrhic War, defeated its southern enemy Carthage in the Punic Wars, and then proceeded to move east, conquering Greece, Asia Minor defeating Antiochus the Great and eventually the rest of the Middle East including Israel.

This Little Horn exalted itself against the Prince of God's host, the Lord Jesus Christ. It then brought an end to the daily sacrifices, destroying Jerusalem and its Temple in 70 AD. Because of Israel's transgressions the Roman Empire was allowed to continue its dominance over the Jews, and to establish a religion Roman Catholicism that casts truth to the ground. No better combination of brevity and accuracy regarding Rome's history

You do not have to drown in despair. No matter who you are, no matter what you have done, God is waiting for you. I pray that you listen for God's voice. If you do, your life will change, your doubt will be removed, and you will believe. I want to take a walk with you someday in paradise, where we can talk about all of these things, where we can receive communication from God, and learn the secrets of His love.

www.ingramcontent.com/pod-product-compliance
Lightning Source LLC
LaVergne TN
LVHW021712060526
838200LV00050B/2628